The myth of HINDU TERROR

Insider account of Ministry of Home Affairs 2006-2010

RVS MANI

Vitasta

Published by
Vitasta Publishing Pvt Ltd
C-29, Sector-7, Noida, Uttar Pradesh - 201301
info@vitastapublishing.com

ISBN: 978-93-86473-27-1

First Edition 2018
12th Reprint 2026

MRP ₹495

Cover and Layout by Somesh Kumar Mishra
Printed by Vikas Computer and Printers

असतो मा सद्‌गमय
तमसो मा ज्योतिर्गमय
मृत्योर्मा अमृतं गमय

This book is dedicated to my parents
Lakshmi and K R Ramaswamy and my
father-in-law K S Venkatachalam who were my
source of inspiration and support,
encouraging me to stand up for the truth.

Contents

Acknowledgements

At the outset I would like to place on record my thanks to Megha Prasad and Aditi Ananthnarayanan of *Times Now*, Prema Sridevi of *Republic TV* and Vasudha Venugopal of *The Economic Times*. The idea of writing a book came from Megha. Prema Sridevi guided me with her professional touch on how the work can be formatted. Vasudha reassured me that I am a good storyteller myself and do not require a script writer. This set off the beginning of this work. My thanks also go to Ms Papri Sri Raman, the editor of this book, for her meticulous efforts in polishing the final version of this book.

My wife Sita has contributed to this in more than one way. She has painstakingly corrected the grammar and checked spellings. My son Aditya, during his home visits from Chandigarh, abandoned the internet and went through the style and presentation. His inputs were indeed valuable.

My erstwhile seniors in the Ministry of Home Affairs have been extremely supportive during my times of tribulations. Special mention for L C Goyal, the then Joint Secretary and currently Chairman and Managing Director of ITPO; D Diptivilasa, IAS (Retd), formerly Joint Secretary in the Ministry of Home Affairs as well as Additional Secretary in the Ministry of Urban Development during my tenure.

Pankaj Kumar Mishra, (IRS-IT), has been a friend, philosopher, guide and shield during my tenure in the MHA as well as after that, when I was going through troubled times. I will always be indebted to him for the support he has extended to me in a very critical phase of my life.

I also thank my former colleagues, S S Das, then Deputy Secretary, MHA, Randhir Singh, former Under Secretary (Naxal Management), MHA, Virendar Kumar, a national-level football referee and my former colleague who was then the Under Secretary, Internal Security and M S Kalaania, also then Under Secretary, Internal Security.

My thanks are also due to Rakesh Singh Nayal, former section officer in the Internal Security Division, as well as T V Paulose, Private Secretary to Director and Sudeesh Negi, PA attached to the office of the Joint Secretary (IS), MHA.

Prologue

The Indian Constitution enshrines in its Preamble itself the principles of secularism. This is undoubtedly the basic tenet of our Constitution. I am restating the Preamble of the Constitution of India below:

> We the people of India, having solemnly resolved to constitute India into a sovereign socialist secular democratic Republic and to secure to all its citizens: justice, social, economic and political; liberty of thought, expression, belief, faith and worship; equality of status and of opportunity; and to promote among them all fraternity assuring dignity of the individual and the unity and integrity of the nation;
>
> In our constituent assembly this twenty sixth day of November, 1949 do hereby adopt, enact and give to ourselves this Constitution.

As a corollary this leads to neutrality. Religious and ethnic neutrality in matters of state and governance. It is meant to be understood that there shall be total neutrality both in perception and in action, in all that the nation does.

But is it true?

Does this happen in reality?

The world over the dictum is: no cause can justify terrorism. Still, in India we have groups, political and nonpolitical, standing up justifying terror acts. They seek pardon for perpetrators of terror acts. They knock at the doors of justices of the apex court with curative petitions after even the President has rejected the pardon.

In a democracy, nonpolitical elite groups doing this can still be tolerated as an anti-view. There is ambivalence on the Right to Dissent which is an offshoot of the Right to Freedom of Expression in such matters. According to Article 19 of the Constitution:

> All citizens shall have the right
> To freedom of speech and expression
> To assemble peaceably and without arms
> To form associations or unions
> To move freely throughout the territory of India
> To reside and settle in any part of India (and)
> To practice any profession, to carry on any occupation, trade or business.

Clause (2) under this Article reads as under:

> Nothing in the sub clause (a) shall affect the operation of any existing law, or prevent the state from making any law, in so far such law imposes reasonable restrictions on the exercise of the right conferred by sub clause (a) in the interest of sovereignty and integrity of India, the security of the state, friendly relations with foreign state, public order, decency or morality or in relation to contempt of court, defamation or incitement to an offence.

In so far as this 'freedom of speech and expression' is concerned, several judicial decisions have confirmed and reinforced in spirit, the right to speech and expression and hence the right to propagate an alternative or dissenting view through media and other sources.

Some of the prominent judicial verdicts have been:

i) Virendra versus State of Punjab, AIR 1958, SC 986
ii) Express Newspapers versus Union of India, AIR 1958, SC, 578
iii) Bennett Coleman versus Union of India, Union of India, 1973, SC 106
iv) Prabha versus Union of India, AIR 1982, SCR 6
v) Indian Express Newspapers versus Union of India, AIR 1986, SC 515
vi) Sakal Papers versus Union of India, AIR 1962, SC 305
vii) Indian Express Newspapers versus Union of India, AIR 1986, SC 872.

In respect of even imposing or introducing any reasonable restrictions by the state also, the government's hands are tied by several judicial pronouncements even if some anti-view (as in these referred-to cases) challenges the objectives set out in the Preamble like challenging the sovereignty and integrity of India. In the following prominent cases the judicial pronouncements are that the burden of proof for imposing these restrictions rests with the state:

i) Vrijlal versus State of MP, AIR 1970, SC 129, 135
ii) Sagir Ahmed versus State of UP, AIR 1954, SC 728
iii) Chintaman Rao versus State of MP, AIR 1950 SCR 759

Further reaffirming and reconfirming this omnibus position—that with further caveat that this Right is unbridled—is the judicial pronouncement which in spirit upheld that reasonable restrictions in the context of this Right applies to both substantive and procedural reasonableness.

Thus, in ordinary circumstances, it is unreasonable to make

the exercise of a Fundamental Right depend on the subjective satisfaction of the executive.

i) Khare versus State of Delhi, 1950 SCR 519, and
ii) Gurbachan Singh versus State of Bombay, 1952 SCR 737

At the same time, I personally hold the view that there are no shades of grey.

But for a sitting government to take sides, abandon neutrality, to ignore facts, to twist facts, to act in oblivion of facts gathered out of painstaking investigation does ring alarm bells in the minds of concerned citizens.

In the process, the government of the day had engineered facts, vitiated the legally-established institutional mechanism to ensure that their narrative gets validated and propagated. However, this is not what the framers of the Constitution ever envisioned.

The so-called 'secular' narrative attempted to be propagated between 2004-2013 had the potential to tear India's social fabric to shreds. In order to reap political benefits, one religious section was projected as overbearing bullies and blamed for certain unfortunate occurrences. To this extent, a nation hostile to the country was partnered. The global narrative was reversed and the victim religious grouping was projected as the oppressor, the perpetrator.

This attempted narrative acted against the very Preamble of the Constitution in letter and spirit. The actions of the then government in power (2009), elected only by virtue of the same Constitution, vitiated the Preamble's objective to 'promote among them all fraternity assuring Dignity of the Individual and the Unity and Integrity of the Nation'.

My tenure in the Union Home Ministry (2006-2010) and the period after that were filled with interesting experiences. In this book I have captured some of these for the people of this country to get a glimpse of how governments work.

Documentation of these events and incidents do exist. In case some are not readily available with the ministry, they can be confirmed from the coordinate institutions like the courts of law, the State government secretariats, police headquarters, books on 26/11, one by the noted journalist Sandeep Unnithan.

In retrospect, my experiences may look 'dire' but I had the inner strength to face the various challenges. My parents had instilled in me this strength. In my younger days I believed that my father, who too was a Home Ministry official, had a tyrannical streak in him. But experiences in my working life made me realise the benefit of rigour which he had insisted we follow while growing up. This rigour, both physical and intellectual, does endow us with capabilities to face challenges.

One lovely and memorable episode I would like to share with readers to reinforce this. One day, I was driving my father through Delhi's Outer Ring Road and was to take a left turn towards Vasant Kunj, near Vasant Vihar Depot. People familiar with the topography will recall that there is a famous south Indian all-purpose store at the turn. My father, at eighty plus, wanted to buy some small utility ware and so I stopped the car before the store. When he returned and my driving resumed, he noticed that I was not wearing a seat belt. He wanted to know why I was not wearing the seat belt? I replied that officers of the Home Ministry are generally not hauled up as the cops identify them from the parking label. He asked me to stop the car, got out in a huff stating that, whether one broke a traffic rule or took someone's life, both were crimes, and he wouldn't travel with a criminal! That is the set of values we have been imbibed with.

Hence, whatever might have been the narrative being authored, engineered, lobbied during my tenure in the Ministry of Home Affairs, I decided that I would stick to the truth. Only the truth. And the interest of my motherland would be paramount and I would not compromise on this. I cannot compromise on this. I have been programmed since childhood to stick to my position, especially in matters that concern my country.

My mother, whom I miss even today, died in the build-up of these challenges, a much-shaken woman fearing for her son's life. I feel a culprit when I think of what she went through. Anyone who had had an opportunity of meeting her will vouch that she was a darling. She had the capacity to shower unlimited love and affection, even on those who might have betrayed her or failed her. This is one value she inculcated in her children. Her memories haunt me, especially when I spill food on my shirt while eating. She would with care wipe it with a wet napkin even when I was 54 years old.

Her loss is unbearable. But I try to console myself that it was all for a cause. For a national cause. For the cause of humanity. What happened to me was perhaps for an ultimate and larger good. I am sure what happened was an aberration, a break in the norm of good governance. I wish no one has to face police harassment in front of his mother like I had to from a CBI DSP Jayant Kashmiri for standing up to the truth.

My parents always knew I stood up for truth on this particular occasion. They knew that I had the courage of conviction. But the CBI DSP, bent on pleasing his bosses, was blinded by ruthlessness and could not see an 87-year old woman witnessing the mental torture he dished out to her son. Although, today I hold no rancour against Kashmiri, at the same time I wish he was brought up with values like those my parents had brought me up with.

My values have also taught me: *Janani Janmabhoomischa swargadapi gariyasi,* meaning, Mother and Motherland are equivalent to heaven.

It's not only in the words. It is in our deeds that each one of us needs to prove ourselves. Even now, when the National Anthem is played, I do stand up. On 30th January, when the siren is blown I stand still as a mark of respect to the Father of the Nation. I have been taught in my school to do so. I have seen my parents, teachers respecting the icons of the nation, respecting the rule of law.

My plea to politicians of this country is that let not such distortions be repeated by any political order just looking for a few votes. Let the law of the land prevail in an environment of justice, good conscience and equity. That's what the fathers of our Constitution envisioned. Let's pledge to actualise their vision of a fair and democratic nation. Whatever may the truth be, let's have the courage to face it and get on with the correction mission.

For this endeavour to really succeed we at first need to know what really happened during those days.

Many observers would have noted a very unique trend in the build-up to the General Elections 2014. Quite a few officers who had served in the security establishments had joined the political group which stood for implementing the objectives of the Preamble to our Constitution. There was R K Singh, former Home Secretary, Satyapal Singh, the former Commissioner of Police, Pune at the time of the German Bakery attack, General V K Singh, the former Chief of Army Staff, Hardeep S Puri, a seasoned diplomat and India's former Permanent Representative to United Nations and many others. On the Economic front also Bibek Debroy, one of the country's leading economists, who, as Director of the Rajiv Gandhi Institute of Contemporary Studies under the aegis of the Rajiv Gandhi Foundation, had acknowledged the success of the Gujarat Development Model had to resign for that. Although this book proposes to detail only the happenings in the security scenario of those days, this example of even the economist being victimised is reflective of the endemic rot that had set in during 2004-2013 in India's governance space.

The dictum to be followed those days was similar to Tennyson's famous poem, *The Charge of the Light Brigade,* that's 'Not to question why, Not to reason why, But to do and die'. It was not just six hundred but many more who were victimised during the Congress-led UPA regime's rule.

It was a Hobson's choice for bureaucrats of the time. You question or change the course, you are doomed, and so is your career. If you pursue with loyalty the then-ruling politicians, your country is doomed. Your professionalism is affected. You will be branded as the 'committed bureaucracy' with all the values you have always stood for, you were given in training institutions, vanquished. It is a process where the civil servants' self-esteem gets demolished bit by bit.

Article 309-311 provides protection and safeguards to the civil servants. But that's only with regard to service matters. There is no protection for your family members, no protection against ostracism by your colleagues, no safeguards against victimisation, no safeguards against delay in career progression etc.

Unfortunately victimisation of this kind happened. That's the reality. I do not intend to wreck vengeance on anyone, whether an individual or a sociopolitical group. I just want to share some of these experiences with the public.

I was ostracised, victimised, chased by the government agencies for standing up for the truth. Some of my less-courageous colleagues avoided me. Some had even stopped taking my phone calls, even official ones. Some suspected my integrity and suspected me of furthering a political agenda.

My impressions about intelligence agencies changed completely after the posting in the Ministry of Home Affairs. Earlier, like a common man, I did not hold the agencies in high esteem, but after being a user of their inputs in my professional life I began to appreciate the quality of inputs they really generate and I, as a citizen, was extremely thankful of their endeavours, efforts and results.

Likewise, after meeting Prema and a few other media personnel my impression about the media professionals changed. They are really good and thorough. At least the media personnel I have met like Prema, Megha Prasad, Aditi, Geeta Mohan, Priyank, Bharti Jain, Manish Shukla and several others.

By 2013, it became obvious that the politically-powerful at that time were getting hit right across the face on account of the stand taken by some of us. Many believed in taking a back seat. Now the attempt is being made to peddle some of the same lies through the route of fiction.

It is really challenging for any civil servant to take on the might of a powerful dispensation. But I have dared to do it. Let us see, how.

Canard or a Sponsored Abhiyaan?

WHILE I WAS in the University of Manchester, a faculty member of Indian origin, Rathin Roy, was working on a theme of dominant coalition. The essence of his theme was that a dominant coalition comprises political elites— 'other governing elites' in the parlance of Italian sociologist Vilfredo Pareto—who are highly-placed public servants and retired public servants serving sinecure, members of the judiciary in coalition with the non-governing elites from corporate houses, media, social activists including NGOs and they form what is known as 'Public Opinion'.

This public opinion, doctored or true, is used as ruse for framing public policy. No matter this public policy is at times at variance with the expectations and requirements of the public at large. Needless to say that every member of this group defined as 'dominant coalition' has his/her own axe to grind in furthering a public policy. This gets validated perfectly in the Indian context.

The Ishrat Jahan story

Recently I read a review of the book *Miss Laila Armed and Dangerous* written by Manu Joseph. The storyline is predictable and seems to reiterate a particular narrative peddled by many in the media.

There is a lot of hype created about dominance and overbearance of people of certain religious grouping that have a major presence, over the others, who do not belong to this group. The author has sought to reconstruct the now well-known Ishrat Jahan case in his work of fiction to reinforce the narrative of how majority manipulation of a minority group took place in the Ishrat Jahan case.

The character akin to Ishrat Jahan is named Laila Armed (the name in the fiction also betrays her ethnicity and Armed is a corrupted form of Ahmed which again is a reinforcement of the faith). Her companion in real life was Javed Mohammed Ghulam Sheik alias Pranesh Kumar Pillai, who was a small-time criminal in Mumbra who converted to Islam for marrying a Muslim woman (not Ishrat). Later, during his stay in the Gulf, this man was radicalised. The location is aptly captured as Mumbra. The IB officer involved, Rajinder Kumar, is given the fictitious character of Mukundan.

The review in *Outlook India* of 23 October 2017 by Saikat Niyogi, titled *Beware of Highwayman,* states: Joseph's novelistic intelligence lies in making Mukundan and Dr Vaid his two most fleshed-out characters. Through them, he plumbs the mental processes—a curious mix of half-truths and unreason—of the Sanghi and the Sangh[1] supporter.

I have not personally known Rajinder Kumar, the senior Intelligence Bureau officer who was victimised by the UPA

---

1 Member of the Bharatiya Jana Sangh, a precursor to the Bharatya Janata Party. It also denotes the supporters of the Rashtriya Swayamsevak Sangh.

government in the Ishrat Jahan case. But I have been exposed to the outputs generated by him. They were precise, accurate and actionable. I have publicly said so in my interview with *Times Now* on 1 March 2016.

IB official Rajinder Kumar had headed the Pakistan Desk in the Intelligence Bureau during his days. He had generated enormous amount of qualitative, precise and actionable inputs. His information had helped liquidate many ISI and Pakistan-sponsored sleeper cells in the country, used to recruit, prepare and arrange logistics for terror attacks in India. Every sleeper cell liquidated meant loss of time, money and resources for the Pakistani establishments controlling these cells. They also suffered collateral damages to their efforts in the jihadi[2] recruitment process amongst local supporters in India.

The Pakistani establishment had cultivated many supporters in the government and other positions, including in the media, who had to prove their loyalties to Pakistan. They had accepted payments in cash or kind, and it was now payback time for the pro-Pakistan Indians. They started a tirade both in the files of the North Block as well as through the judicial process and media against Rajinder Kumar and other loyal countrymen like him.

The image novelist Joseph has portrayed of Rajinder Kumar through his character Mukunadan is criminal, capricious and smells of a larger conspiracy, as does the canard about the Intelligence Bureau per se in the book.

The J&K narrative

I do not think we are a nation of ingrates. But there are people in this country who are now known as 'Libtards, Sickularists' and many other such new terms. Even within these secular brigades,

2 Religious war.

we have positions taken to prove that one group is more secular than the other a la, a detergent ad, *'uski kameez se meri kameez zyada safed'*.[3]

These 'secular' people have for many decades perpetuated a narrative where a majority community becomes the criminal.

Not only Rajinder Kumar or Col Shrikant Purohit et al, but many anonymous innocent honest security personnel, who were defending the nation and were fighting for the ideals of the Preamble of the Constitution, preserving and protecting the integrity, sovereignty and security of India, were painted as 'biased against the minority community'.

At the same time, these very same 'secular' people extended their overwhelming support to many of those who were furthering an agenda of destabilising the nation. These people are known to have given speeches in the United States alleging minority persecution in India.

They used sponsored trips to propagate the anti-national narrative under the garb of human rights, minority rights. They advocated right to self-determination in Kashmir, without having read the Instrument of Accession. They may not have read the 1953 Agreement, and many of the series of agreements between the then Chief Minister of J&K and India. They raised the call of *jihad*. They came out in support of persons who conspired to and attacked the temple of democracy, the Parliament of India. They invoked new remedies for a terrorist, like a Curative Petition, after a Presidential rejection of their clemency plea (this meant, all previous petitions filed in appeal before the Supreme Court and the President of India against the order of the lower judiciary was short on facts).

In my view these people should have been charged for suppression of material facts under Section 218 of the Indian

3 My clothes are whiter than his.

Penal Code. The irony of ironies is that the Supreme Court admitted their petition and heard their plea at wee hours of the morning. After rejection of the curative petition, the sloganeering in a prime institution like the Jawaharlal Nehru University had to be heard to be believed; *'Afzal sharminda hain, tere qatil zinda hai'* was a furtherance of this narrative.

The Binayak Sen story

These people did not bat an eyelid when a CRPF jawan injured in a Naxal attack in Chhattisgarh was denied first aid by a doctor made famous by these libtards. During my tenure in the Ministry of Home Affairs, Battalion No. 82 of the CRPF was posted there. I had met some jawans and officers from this Battalion coming to the Ministry on official errands. They would narrate in detail as to how this local doctor would refuse them first aid in the event of being injured in a crossfire. But the same doctor would extend not just treatment but also hospitality to the Naxals. I have been privy to many papers, conversations and even anecdotes from security personnel serving there at that time.

This doctor and his wife, I was told, allowed their clinic to be used for holding strategy meetings of this criminal group known as Naxals. Spare a thought for the dead Superintendent of Police of Rajnandgaon who was killed by the Naxals. I hold the view that this decorated doctor, Binayak Sen, and his wife Ilina were conspirators. The government in power decorated this conspirator with a plum posting in an advisory role in the then Planning Commission. What were they planning? More such attacks?

The story of the arms loot

It may not be out of context to state here that the Gadchiroli district of Maharashtra was also declared as Naxal-affected at that time. There were many reported ambushes between the Naxals and State Police. Readers can corroborate from the many replies to Questions in Parliament during the period that in many of these ambushes, very few police personnel lost their lives unlike in Chhattisgarh. But every time, policemen's weapons were reportedly snatched by Naxals.

Was it a pattern? Or was it a conspiracy? Or was it a partnership to discredit the neighbouring State government, which was not ruled by the then ruling dispensation at the Centre? Incidentally, Maharashtra was then ruled by the same political dispensation then sitting at the Centre, ie. the Congress Party.

Also it is important to note that whenever police lose their weapons, a procedure is established as per which a court of inquiry-type recording is made. Responsibility is fixed for loss of weapon and some of the policemen are penalised as per the rules of the State. But no such adherence or action was ever reported. *Was the Congress-ruled State government actually helping the Naxals by supplying them weapons by trafficking it through their own police force?* Incidentally, many police personnel posted in those areas will corroborate that in many of the small victories of the security forces in Dantewada, Kanker etc. the weapons seized from the captured and killed Naxals were with police markings.

It is a sheer coincidence that I was in MHA at that time. I got to know the truth. Make no mistake. This is no work of fiction. Every word of informational value can be corroborated from court records, public records which can be accessed through RTI and broadcasts in media etc.

In fact, it was a time when every truth had been replaced by a canard. One of my many objectives in bringing this testimony to light is to demolish narratives being peddled by Manu Joseph's ilk and set the truth before my countrymen.

Journey to the MHA

I HAD BEEN working in the Department of Industrial Development which was rechristened as the Department of Industrial Policy and Promotion.

In 2000, the National Democratic Alliance government had returned to power after demitting office after a 13-month tenure in October 1999. I was posted in the office of the Development Commissioner, Small Scale Industries. A chance meeting in the then UNI canteen during lunch with a gentleman close to B B Ramiah, Member of Parliament, enabled me to offer my services to work with him. The MP had been appointed the Chairman of the MPLADS Committee and I became his Private Secretary. He was a man of erudition and an industrialist of repute. My services were placed on deputation to the Lok Sabha Secretariat in March 2000. I continued with him till he demitted office in April 2004.

In May 2004, the United Progressive Alliance was voted to power. I am not affiliated with any political formation. On my return to my parent unit, I was posted to the Department of Industrial Policy and Promotion in an insignificant placement.

In September 2004, the then government notified the formation of the National Manufacturing Competitiveness Council.

V Krishnamurthy was appointed the Chairman of this Council. He was a past doyen of Public Sector Undertakings who had hitherto served as Chairman of Bharat Heavy Electricals Ltd, Steel Authority of India Limited, Maruti Udyog, Secretary in the Government of India, Member Planning Commission. I was then assigned to work in the National Manufacturing Competitiveness Council and was given the task of setting up the organisation. Unlike other organisations, this Council did not have office space and for nearly three months, another senior colleague with whom I had very close relationship and I operated mostly from the private office of the Chairman in Vasant Vihar.

Thereafter, a Member Secretary was appointed in the Council. He was a retired IAS officer of the 1967 batch. He had retired as Secretary in the Department of Industrial Policy and Promotion. This gentleman, for reasons best known to him, had some sense of caprice and rancour towards me. I was too much of a professional for his attitude to really bother me. Hence the entire year of 2005, I continued to work for the Council. I do not want to reveal the details of daily trials I had to go through during this period as the said person is no more.

However, at a particular point in time, I thought I could not continue here any longer and sought a transfer in my posting. And the transfer came in the form of being posted as Under Secretary in the Ministry of Home Affairs. I thought it was a welcome relief. How was I to know that the future was to hold many more tougher challenges, both professional and personal, particularly in my tenure in the Ministry of Home Affairs? Incidentally, my father had, not long before, retired as Deputy Secretary from the Ministry of Home Affairs. At the time of my MHA posting, he had—call it premonition or foresight—told me that this appointment would be a challenging phase of my work life and I would come out clean and famous.

I began my tenure in MHA by reporting to the Director (Administration) who was a typical bureaucrat who never made anyone feel welcome. Later I learnt that in spite of being empanelled as Joint Secretary, for quite a few years, he had not been picked up as one and this was the reason for his unwelcome behaviour. Having not known the background, I answered his cryptic welcome question with an even more cryptic response. This provoked him. He swore to me that he would post me in a place where no previous incumbent in the last few years had lasted for more than six-to-nine months. Surely, I needed to look forward to this challenging posting. I left my contact number with him, saying, whenever the placement was finalised, he could inform me and I would come and take charge immediately.

Time between postings are periods when people generally attend to their long-pending personal errands, socialise with long lost friends, and even catch up on sleep. I preferred to catch up on sleep and spent time with my ageing parents.

During one of those slumbers, the telephone rang and when I answered, it was the MHA asking me to take over as Under Secretary, Internal Security Division.

I did not have the profile for the job. I reported to the concerned Joint Secretary, who later I came to respect for his erudition, commitment, comprehension and competence. The one virtue that he needed really was the ability to laugh. Notwithstanding this vice, anyone who spent time with him realised that he was not just an able officer; he was an excellent human being. In his own stone-faced style, after assessing me, he started explaining the rules of the game as well as gave me an overview of the work of the Division. At that point, I understood that this gentleman, L C Goyal, had an eye for detail and also demanded full commitment. His demeanour compelled me to assure him of my full commitment at once.

When I took charge of the post, there was one gentleman who had steadfastly lobbied for his way out, who hugged me. Being a senior colleague, I also displayed a sense of warmth towards him. I knew that he had bluffed his way out of the Division by citing illness of his parents and others. So keen was he to be relieved that even the customary briefing was not offered by this gentleman.

I was to share a room with another friend who was a qualified engineer and was dealing with Border Management Projects of the MHA. This is now known as one of the toughest jobs in the country.

Questions in Parliament, IISc blast

After settling the logistical details, when I began to delve into the core functioning of my department, I found that there were questions, motions, calling-attention notices of both Houses of Parliament, of which there was no count, waiting for attention and it was one of my duties to provide the answers and documentation.

Immediate action was warranted in case of many decisions taken in meetings regarding many issues that were pending for a long time. Some work pertaining to the progress of the investigation in the Indian Institute of Science (IISc) bomb blast was also pending. I remember this distinctly because this was the first case I dealt with in the MHA. I knew that long hours of work lay ahead of me.

I had to immediately prepare for disposing of the several assurances that had been made in Parliament in response to various questions/calling attention motions where any Member has the right to call the attention of the government.

Then there were the special mentions which in Lok Sabha are known as Rule 377 cases, in which a Member of any House flags any particular issue which requires the immediate attention of the government. On behalf of the answering authority, the MHA, I had to collate the data in respect of status of the investigation in question. At the very outset, I had to collect information to frame replies to several questions in Parliament as the Budget Session of the year 2006 was on at that time.

Parliamentary questions are of primarily two categories. The simpler one is the unstarred question in which written replies are tendered. The framing of replies is based on information available or collected from various security and other agencies. With due respect to the dignity of the Parliament, bureaucrats refer to this job as *jawab phenkna* (throw the reply).

The starred questions are the ones in which oral replies are tendered by the answering Minister or his deputy. Such a question entitles the questioning Member to ask for two supplementary questions on the subject matter of the question and any other Member of the House can also ask one supplementary question, giving prior notice.

The preparation for not only framing of replies but also anticipating the supplementary questions and their commensurate replies is a very elaborate rigmarole of collecting of information of all possible related areas. Then a separate note for the supplementary is drafted to assist the Minister, which culminates in the briefing session for the Minister and his ministerial colleagues by the concerned bureaucrats. The Internal Security Division always received notices for Questions in dozens and not in ones or twos, on every Question Day.

What is the need for compensation?

More importantly, my purpose of recalling this is to capture the mindset of the then Ministers towards our jawans protecting the borders.

Normally, the briefing session is attended by Deputy

Secretaries/ Directors and personnel of higher ranking. Once, as my Director was not available, I had to stand in for him in one such session. Apart from questions relating to counter-terrorism, there was another one relating to police welfare measures.

Three Ministers were being briefed on the police welfare measures including the compensation for those Central armed police personnel killed in action. At that time I remember, our Minister of State for Home, R R Gavit remarked, what was the need for such compensation, 'since these personnel join the forces for a job and they get paid by way of salary'?

The officers present were shocked. I tried to imagine what if this Minister was asked to go around in a border outpost in the Tangdhar sector in the month of December-January on a visit and inspection between 1 am to 4 am with 17 kilograms of additional burden on his body, including bullet-proof jackets, arms and ammunition, wireless sets etc.

Sikh pilgrims to Pakistan

Every year on four occasions, Sikh *jathas*[4] are sent by the Indian government to various religious places located in Pakistan like the holy Nankana Sahib etc. Since April was approaching, by the time I was in office, jathas to holy shrines in Pakistan on the occasion of Baisakhi, the Sikh New Year, was also to be coordinated. My to do list appeared endless.

The Varanasi bomb blasts

One fine evening, quite late in the evening actually, as I was preparing to leave for the day I received a call from my superior officer. When I reached his office, I was told that there were bomb blasts in Cantonment station and the Sankat Mochan temple in Varanasi. I was told to collect the details from the

4 An armed body of Sikhs the Gurus set up in the 17th century. These Jathas are now processions of pilgrims.

MHA Control Room and draft a statement for the Minister.

After collecting the details, I authored a small statement for the then Union Home Minister Shivraj Patil, to be read in Parliament the next day (in both Houses separately). After culling out the details of the attack, the details of casualties etc. it read: 'I condemn this attack, it is an act of cowardice; I congratulate the people of this country who maintained balance and restraint in this hour of need…blah, blah.' Suffice it to say, both these, the MHA Control Room data input as well as the statement of the Minister, held a lot of importance in presenting this case before the courts.

The significance of this incident is that, after this attack, the frequency of terror attacks increased dramatically and became rather routine occurrences in the hinterlands of India.

For subsequent statements of the Union Home Minister after each later attack, the office of the Minister never asked MHA to draft the statements. The details of the location, time and casualties were obtained and the Minister's office itself issued the statement. However, after the three bomb attacks in Delhi in September 2008, the repetitiveness of the Union Home Minister's statement came in for criticism in the media (*The Pioneer*, if my memory serves me right). They had chronicled the text of the Home Minister's speech after each attack. They asked whether the Home Minister was actually acting to prevent these attacks or he had his 'prepared' statement ready, to be issued immediately after each such attack.

My work for every day was cut out. Getting reports from the MHA Control Room every evening, praying to God that all goes well so that we do not have to stay late in the night etc. At times, I had the company of an excellent and knowledgeable colleague, R Singh who wore only Indian dresses, for guidance and counselling. He was handling anti-Naxal operations while my domain was counter-terrorism and law and order challenges.

Home Secretary-level Talks 2006

The capacity of the Joint Secretary needs to be highlighted here. In 2006, the threat from both, Naxal elements and terrorist fronts, were of high magnitude and the then incumbent officer single-handedly handled both the portfolios very successfully. Now there is a separate Naxal Management Division, with an Additional Secretary, Joint Secretary or Inspector General of Police, three Directors, 4-5 Under Secretaries and staff. Still ambushes happen. Several cooperative mechanisms which were in place at that time are no longer effective.

Like a juggernaut, the Internal Security Division of the country was moving on, getting inputs, sensitising States, sharing intelligence reports etc. There were incidents reported like a low-intensity bomb blast in old Delhi in April 2006, some huge arms seizure at Aurangabad in May 2006 (which is discussed later). And it was time for the 'Home Secretary Level Talks' (HSLT) to be held in Islamabad as a part of a 'Composite Dialogue' process and they were scheduled for 30-31 May 2006.

The previous version of the talks were held in New Delhi. Union Home Secretary V K Duggal was the leader of the Indian delegation in 2006. The Pakistani delegation was led by Syed Kamal Shah, who was scheduled to receive Team India.

We set about preparing for the talks. The compiling of documents for the Home Secretary's opening remarks, the size and composition of the delegation, the logistics, the dossier-sharing rigmarole, coordination between the two countries and various departments and other agencies etc.

On the gifting part, there was a specific input about the Pakistani Interior Secretary's liking for Bikanerwala's Badam Barfi. Hence five kilograms of this was also arranged in addition to other goodies. These were all gift-wrapped. There is a separate Division in the MHA that deals with these matters. What was inside the wrapped packages was not known to us. The delegation left Delhi on 29.5.2006.

Seeding of Hindu Terror

THERE HAD BEEN a huge seizure of arms that occurred between 9-15 May 2006. The amount of arms seized was enough to wage a war against a State.

Details of information received in MHA:

A large number of arms/ammunition including 10 AK-47 rifles, 40 magazines, 200 live cartridges, 10 magazine pouches and 43 kgs of explosive substance including 13 kgs of black colour sticky semi-solid explosive substance were recovered and seized from various parts of Maharashtra such as Aurangabad, Nasik, Beed etc. LeT along with local elements was involved in this case. A chargesheet had been filed against 17 arrested accused under the Maharashtra Control of Organised Crime Act (MCOCA). One accused is on bail. Two more accused were arrested on 4.5.2007 in this case and are in judicial custody. 8 other accused are wanted in this case. One of the main wanted accused, Zabiuddin, was informed to be in Bangladesh. RCN has also been issued against the two wanted accused who are perhaps in Bangladesh. LeT along with ex-members of SIMI are involved in the case.

According to the informal reports that were initially available, the arms were meant for carrying out terror attacks on several sites in Maharashtra including on the RSS headquarters at Nagpur.

Further, there had been terror attacks in Varanasi on 7.3.2006 in the evening on a Tuesday at the Sankat Mochan Hanuman temple, when the place was crowded with devotees. That very evening, another attack had also taken place at the Varanasi Cantt station. This occurred less than an hour before the scheduled departure of the Shiv Ganga Express which carries passengers to New Delhi and en route, the entire western UP is covered by this train. The details of the incident as per available information are:

> Two timer device IEDs, with electric detonators with high grade explosives containing ammonium nitrate and aluminium powder, exploded at Sankat Mochan temple and Cantt. Railway Station, Varanasi on 7 March 2006. One unexploded IED was recovered. 14 persons were killed and 100 injured. HUJAI-BD in association with JeM was involved. Investigation revealed the prime conspirator as Waliullah of Phulpur, Allahabad who aided and abetted the terrorists who came from Bangladesh [he] was arrested and his trial is proceeding. One Mohd Zuber r/o Barod, district Baghpat who was involved was killed in an encounter in Jammu & Kashmir. Three Bangladeshi terrorists namely Bashiruddin, Mustafiz and Zakaria and one Indian, Mohd Shamim of Alinagar PS, Chandauli (UP) are yet to be apprehended and arrest warrants have been issued against them. A chargesheet has been filed against Waliullah on 11.7.2006. The police are continuing to hunt for the absconding accused. RCNs have not been issued against Bangladeshi nationals for want of personal details.

As I had already mentioned earlier, there had been a terror attack in December 2005 in a scientific conference at the Indian Institute of Science at Bangalore in which an emeritus Mathematician of IIT Delhi, Professor M C Puri, lost his life and four other scientists were injured. The brief details of this incident are recalled below:

> An unidentified person lobbed a hand grenade and indiscriminately opened fire from his weapon in the open area in front of the auditorium in the Indian Institute of Science campus on 28.12.2005 killing Prof M C Puri from Delhi and injuring four other delegates. The hand grenade did not explode. The police later recovered one AK-56 Rifle along with four fully loaded AK-56 magazines, four unexploded hand grenades etc.

Prior to this, there had been several terror attacks, like the ones in Delhi on 29.10.2005. Some details of multiple attacks in Delhi on the eve of Diwali festival are:

> Three IEDs with timer device exploded in Paharganj, in a bus at Govindpuri, near Kalkaji and in Sarojini Nagar Market, New Delhi, on 29 October 2005. RDX was used in all three IEDs. 67 persons were killed and 224 persons were injured. LeT was involved in these blasts. There are 8 accused in the triple bomb blasts that occurred in Delhi on 29.10.2005. Out of this, 3 accused, who are Indians, Tariq Ahmad Dar, Mohd. Hussain Fazili and Rafiq @ Mansoor are in custody and have been chargesheeted. The case is being tried in a special court constituted under the provisions of CrPC. Two of the wanted accused, Abu Hufeza and Rashid, have been killed in an encounter. The remaining 3 accused remain at large including Abu Alqama and Zaid. No Red Corner Notices (RCNs) could be issued against them for want of personal details.

Incidentally, all the persons apprehended for these attacks were Muslims. On account of these preceding terror-related incidents, an SMS campaign was triggered: 'All Muslims are not terrorist, but all terrorists are Muslims'. At the time I did not possess a mobile phone. But this is what I received in terms of written inputs.

After this, we got down to preparing for the HSLT 2006, at Islamabad on 30-31 May 2006. All the senior officers of the Internal Security establishment of MHA, officials of Intelligence, Security and Narcotics establishments and the CBI were in Islamabad. They had left Delhi on 29.5.2006 and were expected to return on 1.6.2006.

However, on 1.6.2006, an attack on the RSS headquarters in Nagpur took place. In fact, there had been advisory on this potential attack. It is understood that a senior official of the Intelligence Bureau had personally gone and done a recce of the place and suggested certain safety measures. In spite of that, the attack did occur. Had this senior functionary not carried out the exercise, would the impact of the attack have led to disaster? Partly due to his recce and partly on account of the seizure of arms at Aurangabad from 9-15 May, a disaster was averted.

A few years ago, Seshadri Chari of the RSS had met me at a family wedding. While reminiscing on this event, Chari had told me that left to themselves, the functionaries of this much-maligned organisation were prepared with lathis to counter an attack of this nature, for which the most sophisticated devices were planned to be deployed.

After the RSS headquarters blast

All the officers of Internal Security (IS) Division were in Pakistan in the summer of 2006. I was the only officer present in New Delhi and since my seniors, like the Joint Secretary (IS) whom I had described earlier, and Director (IS) etc. were away, I was taking it easy catching up with a few colleagues over coffee. North Block has an Indian Coffee Board vend where some good authentic decoction coffee akin to what is served in Iyer homes is available. Being posted in Internal Security Division, I was left with little time to really drink my favourite beverage with which we are brought up in Tamil homes. Since it was generally a light day workwise, I was enjoying my coffee at the North Block Coffee House.

At that time, a messenger from the office of the Union Home Minister landed up at the coffee vend, looking for me. Those were the days when the mobile was a sunrise amenity. I did not possess one, hence the messenger came looking for me. I learnt that he had zeroed in on my location after inquiring at several places.

He informed me that I had been summoned by the Additional PS to the Union Home Minister immediately. There was a sense of urgency in his voice and demeanour. I asked him which Additional PS, as full Cabinet Ministers have a sanctioned retinue of 14-15 staff members. He took the name of one Babanagare. This friendly officer had been my colleague in the Lok Sabha Secretariat where I had been on deputation from 2000 to 2004. At that time he was working in the personal establishment of the Speaker. I enjoyed a level of comfort and familiarity with this functionary. Hence, with a relaxed mindset I walked over to his first-floor office from the Coffee House which was also located on the first floor. When I met this Addl Private Secretary, he shoved me into the room of the then Minister, Shivraj Patil.

In government there are these hierarchical protocols which are to be followed. The audibility remaining intact, distance from the chair of the Minister should be directly proportional to your status in the organisation, is an unwritten rule. When an Under Secretary is called by the Minister, which is itself a rarest of rare occasion, firstly he is not to abruptly pull up a chair and sit on it. After being asked to sit, if the Minister so desires, he has to select a chair which is not very close but within the hearing range. Accordingly, I selected a chair and occupied it.

There were two other gentlemen sitting in the room, reclining on the sofa when I entered the room of the Home Minister. There was a familiar air between the three of them. One was a prominent political personality who would in the future overtly come out in support of perpetrators of terror attacks. He had been a former Chief Minister of the State of Madhya Pradesh, belonging to the same party to which the then Home Minister belonged. Of course, for the past decade-and-a-half, this party has not tasted any kind of electoral success in State assembly polls in MP. He had also become a vociferous supporter of certain groups who were in those days accused in terror attacks. Due to this, I could recognise him. He was Digvijay Singh.

The other gentleman sitting in the room was a stranger to me at that point of time. This stranger gentleman asked me about the details of the terror attacks in the then-recent past, what were the casualties, what was the then status of investigation(s) for each etc. From his demeanour and way of seeking information, I could deduce that he was a police officer. Much later during my tenure in the Ministry of Home Affairs, I could identify this officer. He unfortunately got killed in the 26/11 attacks. He was Hemant Karkare.

Thereafter, Digvijay Singh asked me for some more information.

I also informed them that other senior officers of the department would be arriving in Delhi from Islamabad in a few hours (of 1st June) but that submission of mine was not taken cognisance of. They were not even interested in knowing when the Home Secretary would be returning. During the whole interaction, the Home Minister appeared unconcerned and laid back while presiding over the 'seeking of information' by the other two individuals.

From the intermittent conversation between the two individuals in the Minister's room it was clear that they were not happy with my information that 'a particular religious group was involved in most of the terror attacks'.

However, this was what the investigating agencies were furnishing the Internal Security Division with, as I had no other source of intelligence. But from the deliberation in the Home Minister's Office it was clear that they were not happy with the intelligence input that Muslims were aiding terrorists. The way the information was sought from me made it very obvious that the source of this input was being deeply evaluated. There were repeated references to Nanded, Bajrang Dal etc. in their conversation.

The Nanded Affair

The first seed of the canard—that Hindus were also terrorists—was sown with this case. Until then, we had not heard the word 'Hindu terror'.

However, at the time of the 1st June discussion in Patil's office, my department in IS had no information about any terror attack in Nanded. The incident had happened, I later learnt, a week before. We also did not have any information on Bajrang Dal in the Internal Security Division. It was in the domain of the Human Rights and National Integration (HR/NI) Division of the Ministry of Home Affairs. This Division was then located in the Lok Nayak Bhavan, Khan Market, in New Delhi at a distance of about 6 km from the North Block. Since there was no specific information sought on anything related to Nanded or Barjrang Dal, I kept quiet.

As per the laid-down procedure in such contingencies, I reduced the interaction in the Minister's office to writing a report for the knowledge of my seniors and forgot about it. This report was submitted on 1st or 2nd of June 2006. I am sure if one scrounges the records of the period in the Internal Security Division, the copy of the document will be available if it has not met the shredder in the meantime. One can also corroborate the existence of such a report at the relevant time, because in Internal Security Division my staff always kept a diary of papers generated and submitted by me and so did the staff attached to my seniors. Surely, even if one diary of those times is available, one can confirm the existence of my submissions.

More importantly, the bonhomie between the two individuals other than the Home Minister was great and very visible. It may be interesting to recall that Digvijay Singh had later claimed in a media report that he was in personal touch with the police officer who was in the room of the Union Home Minister along with him at that time and obtained specific information on the Nanded attack. Singh had also declared the personal mobile number of this police officer in the media. This can be verified from media reports.

What was intriguing, which no one from the media or otherwise at that time asked, was: what was the relationship between a political leader and an Indian Police Service Officer of a neighbouring State cadre? Indeed, having been the Chief Minister of a State, Singh might have known many a police officer from his own State. But to be so friendly with a serving IPS officer of a neighbouring State is something that begs an answer. *Without imputing motives to any individual, what was the police officer doing with a politician of a neighbouring State?* AIS Conduct Rules expressly proscribe general hobnobbing of All-India Service personnel with political leaders except in discharge of functions.

Immediately after, within a few days, a 'Hindu Terror' case came on records. One Sameer Kulkarni of Nanded was allegedly storing explosives in his workshop, which exploded on 20.4.2006. Later, the case was handed over to the CBI. In the investigation, it was found that Kulkarni was actually running some small business in his workshop and as is generally prevalent, when there is lull in business in small towns, some people set fire to their workshops to make a false insurance claim. As per reports, Kulkarni used to also visit the Bajrang Dal office in Nanded.

The supervisory officer and senior management of CBI, however, refused to change their findings. An officer, who was tipped to be the next Director of the CBI, was penalised and not made the Director. There was no charge framed in this case by the CBI and the case was brought to an abrupt end. However, the facts can be verified from the media reports of the time.

The Sabarmati Express narrative

It may look out of place, but this is also a rebuttal to Sanjiv Bhatt, IPS, who said that he was attending a meeting in the Chief Minister's chamber on 28.2.2002. Often Bhatt has falsely claimed to have been present in a meeting chaired by the then Chief Minister of Gujarat (now Prime Minister Narendra Modi) on the day after the unfortunate incident of burning of some sleeper coaches of the Sabarmati Express at the Godhra Railway Station.

Bhatt has alleged that this meeting was attended by the Additional Chief Secretary (Home), Principal Chief Secretaries, Commissioners, Inspectors General, DIGs etc. Sanjiv Bhatt has alleged that the Chief Minister had directed the officers to 'let the Hindus vent their anger'. I can aver that Bhatt is blatantly lying.

In case such a meeting was ever held and he was in attendance, in the meeting obviously the front rows would have been occupied by the Additional Chief Secretaries, Principal Secretaries, Director General of Police, Additional Directors General of Police, and in any space still unoccupied by higher-ranking officials, there may be seated one or two Secretaries/ Commissioners/ Inspectors General etc.

Anyone who is conversant with hierarchical protocols and

conventions of bureaucracy can visualise the location of Bhatt in the meeting room and his distance from the Chairman of the meeting. Also, despite conference microphones being available, the audibility of the Chair's observations would have been extremely weak to a person sitting in Bhatt's purported hierarchical location, given the general vice in government conference rooms where the previous speaker almost always forgets to switch off the mike, making the observation of succeeding speakers almost inaudible. It is on the basis of my long experience as a government official that I am questioning Bhatt's statement that the then CM had said what Bhatt alleges, he did.

Furthermore, my long innings in civil service has also taught me that every meeting is minuted. The said meeting would also have been minuted and the minutes would have contained the list of persons attending the meeting. This list is captured through an attendance sheet circulated in every such meeting. This sheet is also circulated in the first row first, and in that serial order. Hence, the order of the names of attendees in the list also, in a broad sense, reflects the distance from the Chairman of the meeting. People may rest assured that in case any civil servant is found throwing about any proximity to any Minister, he is surely lying. We have a lot of them in Delhi known as 'powerbrokers' with a common refrain that 'so-and-so was drinking in my flat'.

The rights of Dakini-Chakini

Was Nanded the first such story planted in the pliant media? Manifestly yes. Throwing direct accusations, I believe yes. However, the majority community has been indirectly tarnished for long.

At the time he was the Chief Minister of the combined State of Madhya Pradesh and Chhattisgarh, Digvijay Singh was no innocent. One part of the State of Chhattisgarh to date continues to be ravaged by Naxal violence as an aftermath of his policies.

Great hermit and seer Agastya, in his southern quest, had come across two rivers which were revered as Mother Goddess. They were as much revered as mother Ganga. These two rivers are called Chakini and Dakini. In his famous work *Lalitha Sahasranamam* (1000 praises to the Goddess), the Goddess mother is referred to as *Chakiniamba swaroopini* (she who adopts the form of *Chakini*) and also *Dakiniswari* (she who is the Goddess form of *Dakini*). They flow in Chhattisgarh. These two rivers are vital source of supply of not just water to the community there. A lot of livelihood issues of the local community were linked to these two rivers.

A central public sector undertaking, the National Mineral Development Corporation (NMDC), had started its mining activities in the region. These are known as the Bailadila Iron Ore Mines, Bacheli, Kirandul and Donimalai Mines. Effluent from these mines were dumped in these rivers over a period of time. Digvijay Singh, who was Chief Minister in 2000-2001, was reportedly flagged on this. No redeeming action was taken on the part of this political leader as Chief Minister. The waters in these rivers became poisonous over a period of time due to unabated dumping of toxins.[5] The local community protested and when their grievances were not mitigated, the attendant

---

5 Maureen Nandini Mitra, *Downtoearth*, Center for Science and Environment Sunday 31 December 2006 reported:

Rivers Shankhini and Dankini in Chhattisgarh run dirty. There have been some attempts to address the situation, but none have been followed through to the end. In 1990, the Union government's science and technology cell reported that reckless exploitation of the mines and release of effluent into the rivers had damaged not just the rivers but also 35,000 hectares of agricultural and forest land around Bailadila. People from about 100 villages used the polluted Shankhini and Dankini waters for their daily needs. Four years later, the then Madhya Pradesh government declared that 65 villages along the Shankhini and Dankini were affected by the polluted waters and ordered NMDC to dig some 200 wells to provide safe drinking water for these villages. The wells were dug all right but were too shallow, not one of them is functional today. NMDC officials, of course, don't have to worry about their drinking water.

unrest was violent, the aftereffects of which are still being felt in the region.

No Medha Patkars, Arundhatis, Aruna Roys, Priya Pillais, Harsh Manders and other human rights advocates ever took up the issues of the local people here as there was no funding for any protests here. Surely livelihoods could be lost. '*Bhaar mein jaaye livelihood. Bhaar mein jaaye human rights. Apne ko roti sekni hai, woh bhi secular roti.*'

The bulldozing of this particular project was surely a force multiplier, aggravating the Naxal problem in the region. One of the human rights activists active in the Naxal region and who is an academic, Bela Bhatia, is known for her tirade against the local government as well as the present union government (both under BJP rule). One of her premise is, human exploitation is the reason for problems plaguing the State of Chhattisgarh. Her husband, Jean Drèze, has been a member of the powerful National Advisory Council during the UPA regime. He did nothing in this regard. Was this just omission or was this by design to give Naxals an excuse?

These cases are not closed yet

THE LACK OF involvement of the top brass in security issues can be gauged from the fact that the scourge of fake currency being circulated through many ATMs all over the country were being reported since 2006. MHA had many inputs on this. But the first concrete standard operating procedure (SOP) was devised after a new Home Secretary, Madhukar Gupta, took over in June-July 2007.

It took another six months of elaborate work by MHA on his initiative and only in January 2008 were the State governments finally ordered to take concrete steps to control this menace. The irony of the times was such that in 2006-07, both, the Union Home Minister and Union Home Secretary, appeared unconcerned with security matters. Their involvement did not appear total. We had a committed L C Goyal as Joint Secretary in the Internal Security Division and G S Rajagopal as an excellent Special Secretary (Internal Security), positions always earmarked for two of the most senior IPS officers in the country. I do not know whether they were delegated the authority to take decisive action or they were also struggling to really be heard by the Home Minister and the Home Secretary. But the Special Secretary shortly seized his opportunity to get a posting as Director of Sardar Vallabhbhai Patel National Police Academy, a position befitting his erudition. We always imagined him more as a professor than as a police officer.

I, therefore, had to learn my first steps on the 'reactive action to be taken' in the event of a terror attack in a real time situation. I cut my teeth with the 11 July incidents. But the 11.7.2006 Mumbai train attacks were only the beginning.

Mumbai 11/7/2006 and aftermath

Ill exposed as I may have been to handling the documentation and gazetting of any terror attack at the time of Varanasi in March 2006, I was to meet these challenges very soon.

On 11 July 2006, seven serial blasts occurred in the First Class compartments of Mumbai suburban trains causing death of 187 people (including one Pakistani who had planted the bomb) and injuries to about 872 people.

> The Mumbai police Anti-Terrorist Squad (ATS) chargesheeted 13 Indian nationals on 30 November 2006 for these serial blasts. All these 13 accused have been arrested by the police. Subsequently, on 1 December 2006, 15 wanted accused (10 Pakistanis and 5 Indians) were chargesheeted. The MCOCA designated court, Mumbai has issued Non Bailable Warrants against these 15 absconders. Out of these 15, Red Corner Notices have been issued against Rahil Sheikh and Rizwan Mohammad Dawrey. One Pakistani who was involved in the case was killed in a police encounter in Mumbai.

These are facts available in the police records, court records and public domain. But what is salient here and needs to be noted is that it took nearly five months for the ATS, which was directly mandated to investigate and identify the perpetrators, to do their jobs. This particular timeline is revisited while I detail the performance of the same ATS in the Malegaon (2008) case.

I had left the office at the time the 11.7.2006 train attack reports came in. Joint Secretary Goyal, who was in office when the reports came in, had gone over to Mumbai that night itself and returned to Delhi in the morning. He had reported directly to the office. I was not very sure of my exact role in the aftermath. When I reached office on 12.7.2006 morning, he called me into the office and briefed me in detail on the action to be taken. In fact, since he had not slept in the night, when he told me that the survivor information could be had from the K B Bhabha Hospital, I misheard the name and he was irritated due to lack of sleep.

The Director (IS), P K Mishra, had gone to Japan for a workshop on biological terrorism and was expected to be in Delhi not before 14.7.2006. Knowing our excellent relationships, the Joint Secretary tersely told me to get the job done as quickly as possible. More than being reported to my Director, it was my esteem at stake. I collected and collated every information regarding the train attacks, the casualties, the survivor information, the possible evidences left behind, the progress reported by the State police (ATS etc.) as first respondents to the event, the details of documentation they had etc. and also internally looked at whether any input had been received from our sister agencies, any sharing of the inputs through general or specific advisories etc. I collected all these detailed information and put them together in a report for the Joint Secretary as he had desired.

After thorough examination and two or three returns for correction, confirmation and modification, this report was sent to the office of Special Secretary (IS), Rajagopal, the Union Home Secretary and the then Home Minister.

Malegaon after Mumbai

In the immediate aftermath of the Mumbai train attacks came the Malegaon incidents in September of the same year.

Original information received from the State police was that it was the handiwork of an extremely orthodox Islamic group known as Ahl-e-Hadith (known in India as the Ahl-e-Hadees). This was the first time I had heard of such a sub group within Islamic society. This group is said to live by the edicts of Islam and by the shariat law. They are committed to the establishment of Islamic order and Islamic state in India and the world over. I do not know whether the present ISIS is an extension of this Ahl-e-Hadith. The preliminary inquiry by the local police had concluded that Malegaon was the work of Ahl-e-Hadith.

If I remember correctly, on 8.9.2006, our full team was present in the department. By this time, I too had become familiar with the procedures of acquiring information. On this occasion, I directly obtained all the information from the SP (Rural), Nashik, Maharashtra. According to information obtained from the Police Department of Maharashtra, as per the confessions of those arrested, the accused persons belonged to the Students Islamic Movement of India, SIMI, a banned organisation.

> *Initial information received:*
>
> On 8.9.2006, four bomb explosions occurred in Malegaon which resulted in the killing of 31 persons and injuries to 312 persons. 9 persons have been arrested in this case and 4 others are absconding. A chargesheet was filed on 21.12.2006 by the ATS Mumbai against the accused persons. According to the confessions, the accused persons belong to SIMI, a banned organisation. There were riots in Malegaon in 2001-02 in which the Muslim community suffered and police allegedly acted against them, as per their confessions. The accused, therefore, conspired to take revenge from the police, Government and the other community and decided

> to get weapons from abroad. After the Mumbai blasts of 2006, RDX and other implements for making bombs were brought from Mumbai to Malegaon. The occasion for these blasts was carefully chosen so as to incite communal riots in Malegaon. The two arrested accused namely, Shabir Masiullah and Sheikh Mohd Ali Alam Sheikh, had been to Pakistan for weapons training in 2006. The case is now being investigated by CBI. The investigating agency has one eye-witness to the case and one of the accused has turned approver. CBI is seeking the sanction of the competent authority under MCOCA and Unlawful Activities (Prevention) Act, 1967 as amended in 2004 (UAPA) for the special court to take cognizance of the case.

The information above are also available in the police records, court records and public domain. In addition, now and then, different bits of evidences/records of these have been displayed/quoted in various national news channels like *Times Now*, *Republic TV*, *NewsX* etc. The famous Nagori (of SIMI) tapes which were telecast reinforces this.

Samjhauta Express blast

This was followed by the Samjhauta Express blast. This was internationally noticed as this particular train service was started as a symbol of amity between the two feuding neighbours. In this case, I obtained the first-level information from SP (Railways and Crime) Panipat, Haryana.

> *The initial revelations*:
>
> On the intervening night of 18/19-2-2007 at about 11:40 pm there was a blast in train No. 4001 Samjhauta Express (Delhi to Attari) in which two bogies were burnt near Diwana, (Panipat) in Haryana. As a result of which 68 passengers died and 12 others were injured. Only 48 bodies could be identified out of which 39 were Pak nationals and 9 Indians. A case FIR No.28 dated 19-02-2007 u/s 302/307/124-A/438/446 IPC and u/s 3/4/6 Explosives

Act 150/151/152 Railway Act u/s 3 and 4 of Prevention and damage of public property Act has been registered in Police Station GRP, Karnal. During checking, two live time bombs were recovered in two different suitcases along with bottles of kerosene oil, which were disposed off by the Bomb Disposal Team. A special investigation team was constituted. The evidence from the blasts site of Samjhauta Express led the Police to Indore, Madhya Pradesh, from where they also detained two persons from whom the terrorists had purchased the bags/covers in which the bombs were placed. However, no further lead could be given by these two detained persons, hence they were released.

A Karachi-based terrorist outfit claimed responsibility for the attack at that time. A special investigation team was constituted. In June 2016, in *NewsX*, the first responder to the event, Bharti Arora, IPS, then SP (Police and Railways) of Panipat, confirmed the finds. Recently, the Inspector who is the investigating officer in the case has also reaffirmed this on television. These are the confirmations available in the public domain. The Nagori narco tapes, which were also telecast by *Times Now,* reaffirms this position.

Interestingly, there is a reference to the Samjhauta blast case included in the series of dossiers shared with Pakistan on every bilateral mechanism. Isn't this an official acknowledgement of Pakistani involvement? Basically, the dossier is entitled, 'Dossier on fugitives from Indian law living in Pakistan'.

The then official position (in 2007) was that this attack was carried out by an Indian group and some Indians had to stand trial for it (Sameer Kulkarni, Pragya Bharati, Purohit, Aseemananda and others). *If that was the position, then why did this incident get included in the Pak dossier?* The box of paradox explodes in the face of the then government when answers are sought to my questions. This would perhaps accord a clear opportunity to Pakistanis to grandstand. Or was it an escape route being offered to Pakistan to get away with the charge of fermenting terror in India, because anyone can ask these questions.

Mecca Masjid blasts

Initial information obtained:
On May 18, 2007 a bomb blast took place in Mecca Masjid near Charminar in Hyderabad wherein 9 persons were killed and 58 others injured. The case is now being investigated by the Central Bureau of Investigation. CBI has reported that the inquiry in respect of the SIM Card found in the mobile phone used in the unexploded device has revealed that it was issued in West Bengal. The person in whose name the SIM Card was issued and the address given at the time of application of the SIM Card were found to be non-existent. The driving licence given as a proof of identity was also found to be forged. The investigation has also revealed that other SIM Cards have also been purchased using similar forged ID proofs. Enquiry has also revealed that the mobile phone instrument was purchased from Faridabad and further enquiry in this regard is being made. A reward of Rs 2 lakh has been declared for information on the blast. It is further informed that a number of SIM Cards were procured by those involved in the case on the basis of fake ID proofs from Jharkhand and West Bengal. It has been gathered that Mohd. Shahid @ Bilal, a resident of Hydrabad and LeT/JeM activist was behind this incident and that the explosive was placed by one Hamza @ Kanchan @ Sharifuddin, a Bangladeshi who is also wanted in a case by Delhi police.[6]

These are information available in public domain, in the court records of the Special CBI Judge at Hyderabad. Certain

6 Five accused, including former Rashtriya Swayamsevak Sangh (RSS) member Aseemanand, were acquitted by a special NIA court in Hyderabad on 16 April 2018. Nine persons were killed in the blast that was carried out using an improvised explosive device.

similarities between the Samjhauta Express blasts and the Mecca Masjid blast were noticed in so far as both used batteries of 6 volts and cast iron pipes etc.

Lumbini Park at Hyderabad on 25.8.2007

Initial details obtained:

Two blasts occurred in quick succession around 8 pm on 25.8.2007, one at Lumbini Park and the other at Gokul Chat Bhandar in Hyderabad. A total of 43 persons were killed and 69 were injured (Lumbini Park – 12 dead, 18 injured. Gokul Chat Bhandar 31 killed, 51 injured).The case is being investigated by Hyderabad Police. Mohammad Shahid @ Bilal is believed to be behind these blasts also. As per the reports of the Hyderabad Police, the investigation is being conducted by the Special Investigation Team, Hyderabad. There is strong suspicion of involvement of HUJI cadres of Bangladesh along with local modules. Elaborate efforts have been made by Hyderabad Police to identify and examine the local suspects. In this process, 70 persons have been examined. This includes 22 Bangladeshis residing in Hyderabad. During the process of examination of the suspects, while evidence of their complicity in the twin blasts could not be gathered, evidence against 26 persons has been found regarding their involvement in other offences like obtaining multiple SIM Cards under fake identity for carrying on subversive activities, trying to procure passports on fake identity, possessing Jehadi literature, entering into conspiracy to wage a war against the State and bringing RDX etc. For these offences, five separate cases were booked. In these five cases, 26 persons have been arrested. The investigation was done by using scientific methods and tests like lie detector, brain mapping and NARCO analysis. Further investigation is being carried out in coordination with investigating agencies of other States like Maharashtra and Rajasthan as well as the central intelligence agencies.

These are again information available on public domain, in the court records of the Special CBI Judge at Hyderabad.

Ajmer Sharif

Details of the incident are as follows:

On 11.10.2007 evening, a blast occurred in the premises of Ajmer Sharif at Ajmer. In this blast 3 civilians were killed and 14 others injured. The triggering of IED containing low intensity explosive and iron pieces, apparently done by a cellphone. One of the deceased by name Sayeed Salim reportedly from Hyderabad who came to Ajmer about 7-8 years ago, who used to be a passport agent, is said to be a suspect. There are a lot of similarities between this blast and the blast at Mecca Masjid in Hyderabad that occurred on 18.5.2007, in terms of the device/cell-phone and explosives used, the piece of the newspaper in which the device was wrapped, the unexploded device etc. So far, no arrests have been made in the case. No arrests have also been made so far in the investigation of the Mecca Masjid blast, which is now with CBI. Indications are that in both these blasts, Shahid Bilal, an LeT/HUJI activist who is from Hyderabad and is presently supposed to be in Karachi and the combination of cadres of LeT and HUJI-BD seem to be involved.[7]

The shared dossier

I have placed portions of the dossier shared by the Indian Foreign Office with Pakistan in January 2009 after the Mumbai attack before my readers. I have also recalled reference to the previous documents so shared in different bilateral mechanism like Home Secretary Level Talks, Joint Anti-Terror Mechanisms etc. The

---

7 A special court in Jaipur on 8 March 2017 acquitted Aseemanand and six others in the case of the 2007 Ajmer Dargah blast that killed three persons and injured 17. Three others were convicted by the court. The NIA did not contest the finding.

dossier/s has been accessed from the internet. The dossier excerpts are quoted on the as-is-where-is basis in the chapter on 26/11. Mohammad Bilal alias Shahid Bilal's name appears repeatedly in all the dossiers shared in different bilateral mechanisms with Pakistan.

District court premises at Jaunpur, Faizabad and Varanasi

This is an interesting case. MHA had forewarned the State government through an advisory regarding the possibility of blasts in many court premises in Uttar Pradesh, based on intelligence inputs in mid-October 2007. Later, this advisory was reiterated in a second advisory in the first week of November 2007. I do not know whether the State government took any necessary preventive steps. But the blasts occurred in three places on 21.11.2007.

I had filed a detailed affidavit in the Allahabad High Court on 4-5 January 2008, when the High Court had taken suo motu cognisance of the security of court premises and asked the Union of India to file their response. Specific and actionable intelligence had been shared over many months with the government of Uttar Pradesh. In this context, another relevant extract which I recall from the Affidavit filed in Allahabad High Court in the court security case is:

> The Ministry of Home Affairs vide its communication dated 4.6.2007 forwarded a copy of the guidelines for the security of High Courts and District/Subordinate Courts to all State governments and Union Territory Administrations with the request to urgently review the security arrangements of the High Courts and District/Subordinate Courts and adequately strengthen them to avoid any untoward incident.
>
> i) An advisory was issued to all the State Governments on 4th June 2007 inter-alia mentioning that terrorist elements remained quite active and had used sleeper

cells in the hinterland of the country. In the alert, while reiterating the Central government's commitment to extend all possible assistance through real-time sharing of intelligence and coordination, the State governments were advised to maintain utmost vigilance on all vulnerable targets and to activate local police and intelligence agencies for gathering information on suspect groups and take effective counter measures.

ii) Further, another advisory was issued on 18.7.2007 to all States and UTs about the possibility of retaliatory strikes in view of continuing relationship between the underworld and terrorist groups. The State governments were advised to consider adequate security arrangements against attacks in busy crowded places including trains/buses, institutes of iconic fame etc.

iii) More recently, two advisories were issued to State authorities in October 2007, alerting the State authorities about plans of terrorist groups to carry out attacks during important religious festivals and congregations. It was also mentioned that adequate access control measures should be put in place to thwart such plans.

iv) During recent meetings held between the agencies of UP and the Central government to review the security arrangements at Mathura on 16.10.2007, Taj Mahal on 17.10.2007, Ayodhya on 15.11.2007 and Varanasi on 16.11.2007, the State government was sensitised on the linkages of certain terrorist groups in UP and possibility of targeting of crowded areas by terrorist groups. However, there was no specific prior input regarding the serial blasts in Court premises in UP that happened on 23 November 2007.

A sleeper cell, headed by one Haji sahib—I do not exactly recollect the name—from Phulpur or Pratapgarh near Allahabad was alleged to be behind the blasts. The case was investigated by the STF, located in Lucknow. The chargesheet was filed by UP Police STF in the relevant Lucknow Court.

CRPF Camp Rampur

> *The dawn of 2008*
> On 1.1.2008, at about 0230 hrs. 3-4 terrorists attacked CRPF Group Centre at Rampur with automatic rifles and hand grenades. As a result, 08 persons (07 personnel and 01 civilian) were killed while 05 persons (03 CRPF personnel, 01 local police-man and 01 Home Guard) were injured. Seven persons were arrested in this case. The primary reasons for [this was] some encroachments inside the CRPF campus that the force had been taking up with the State authorities but to no avail.
>
> 7 persons Imran Shahzad @ Abu Shama of Lashkar-e-Taiba, Muhammad Farooq Bhatti @ Abu Zaar of Lashkar-e-Taiba, Sabahuddin Ahmad @ Farhan of Lashkar-e-Taiba, Muhammad Sharief @ Suhail of Lashkar-e-Taiba were involved in the attack on CRPF camp at Rampur- on January 01, 2008.
>
> This incident is also mentioned in the Indo-Pak dossier.

Modasa

Tauseef Khan alias Mohammad Atiq, an Indian Mujahideen, was found to be the perpetrator. He was from a sleeper cell operating in Bihar. He had the support of SIMI volunteers including someone called Ghulam Khan or Saravar Khan. These persons, as per my latest information, have been convicted.

Delhi blasts and Batla House

Blasts occurred in Delhi in three places in September 2008. They were traced to the doors of some Azamagarh-based radicalised groups that were reportedly involved in these blasts. It is well reported that when the police went to investigate the same in Batla House in Shaheen Bagh, Jamia Nagar, New Delhi, these terrorists killed one of the best special cell personnel. This Inspector, Mohan Chand Sharma, had an illustrious record to his credit of neutralising sleeper cells/ fake networks etc.

The encounter was investigated by the then Joint Commissioner (Crime), Amulya Patnaik who later on went on to become the Commissioner of Police. He had also found after inquiry that it was a cross-fire that had killed Sharma, the special cells police inspector.

Shivraj Patil, the Union Home Minister, was present in Delhi Police Headquarters to inaugurate a facility on 19 September 2008, when the Batla House encounter was happening. He was briefed on a concurrent basis. He would have also been privy to wireless messages coming to and fro. But he chose to keep quiet when his colleagues questioned the encounter as 'fake'. Especially the prominent politician Digvijay Singh, whom I had met in the Home Minister's chamber two years ago, the one who was pioneering this theory of fake encounters. It was not without reason. It is a different matter that in spite of the court also upholding the cross-fire evidence, this politician continues to harp that Batla House was a 'fake encounter'. The Order of the court is also in public domain.

The Mumbai ATS

Surely the 'fake encounter' theorists got the much-needed oxygen from both, the Union and the State governments, when the investigation got a twist to suit the 'Hindu terror' narrative.

By mid-2008, the Anti-Terror Squad of the Maharashtra police began to take over the Malegaon and other investigations within Maharashtra, almost two years after the incidents. Law and Public Order are State subjects under Schedule VII of the Indian Constitution. Hence, the State government is well within its power to assign the investigations to any agency, whether crime branch or ATS as they deem fit

At the same time, assignment from the investigating agency with natural jurisdiction to another specialised agency is carried out after an elaborate laid-down procedure of approvals. There was a speed and alacrity with which the Malegaon case was taken out of the local police jurisdiction and assigned to the ATS. No one questioned that move. The Union of India could not question the decision.

When I had marked and paged the timeline in the case of the Mumbai local train attacks earlier, I had deliberately highlighted that the ATS, Mumbai had taken five months to identify the perpetrators of the attack. Generally, that is the benchmark. Such complicated cases do require the *de rigour* to be gone through so that the right persons are arrested.

The ATS was headed by Hemant Karkare whom I had seen in the Home Minister's room two years ago, conceiving in collusion with a political leader, a strategic narrative counter to Islamic terror by authoring a 'Hindu terror' narrative.

Immediately after the taking over of the Malegaon probe by the ATS, the narrative changed.

The involvement of Ahl-e-Hadith/Hadees in the incident was trashed. Again, it may be iterated that law and public order are State subjects. Hence the Ministry of Home Affairs can only accept the status as provided by the State police or its relevant branch. We can sit on judgment over its conclusions and deductions but we can do little else. Reports were received from Mumbai about involvement of certain Hindu organisations in the attack. I do not know what the ground realities were and whether the motorcycle (the so-called evidence in the case) was planted etc. in the Malegaon evidence record. Some Sadhvi Pragya, Shivnarayan Kalsangra etc. were reported to be the brains behind the attack. Surprisingly, everyone lapped up the story as 'gospel truth' without examining the evidence and the records of the other events.

It is a matter of record that in the Mumbai 11.7.2006 cases, it took almost five to six months when the investigation was in a straight line for the ATS to arrest the suspects. In Malegaon, it took just 35 days for the same ATS from the date of occurrence to arrest a serving Indian Army Officer, Lt Col Shrikant Prasad Purohit. In these 35 days, some time would have also been lost in the procedural work involved in transfer of the case to ATS. More time would also have been lost in getting the required clearances from the Defence Headquarters for imputing the charges on a serving defence officer. Hence, it is hard to digest that in less than a month, wisdom dawned on the ATS that Malegaon was the handiwork of Hindu terror groups, although the field-level police personnel of the range continued to report that Ahl-e-Hadith/ Hadees was involved.

I would always suggest that interested readers speak to some of the local police personnel of the time who have by now retired. Many of those retired policemen have settled in Malegaon or Nashik city. Once, on a visit to Nashik, I did stroll through the road from Dwarika Hotel Chowk towards the west of the city which leads to certain congested parts. I spoke to some fellows in a chai shop where some of these retired persons generally come for an evening chat. While I did not identify myself, my inquisitiveness made people feel I might be from the media, so I had to settle my chai bill quickly and hurry back to the hotel.

At a time when we had the best team in the IS Division of the MHA, the attitude of the government in power and intent to colour every terror incident as 'saffron' and their ambivalence in acting against the real perpetrators of the terror attacks was making this country a cannon fodder for those with evil designs against India.

The 2008 HSLT

It was also about that time that the next edition of the Home Secretary-level Talks with Pakistan were to be held. The mutually convenient date had been fixed for 25 November 2008. Home Secretary Madhukar Gupta had asked us to identify the items to be put on the table. Accordingly, we had commenced our consultation process with the security agencies and other Divisions of the MHA and other Ministries like the MEA. The composition of the delegation was being finalised. Like every edition, this time also the composition was the same.

The delegation was to leave by a BSF aircraft while the Home Secretary was to be accompanied by the then Deputy Secretary (Pakistan). They were to travel by road from Amritsar to Attari on 23 November to oversee the Immigration establishment, and from there to Lahore and on to Islamabad.

The delegation was constituted as per convention, which included apart from different agency representations, the Home Secretary as leader, officers in charge of Internal Security, Foreigners etc. Anwar Ehsan Ahmad, Additional Secretary (Border Management), was included. In this context, I would like the readers to recall the composition of delegation in the 2006 edition. Inclusion of this Additional Secretary (Border Management) was unconventional and unprecedented in the HSLT with Pakistan.

At the same time, there was a notice for contempt of court received by the Union Home Secretary. It related to some UP sugar scam and the petitioner was one Vishwanath Chaturvedi. This was in no way the concern of the Ministry of Home Affairs. However, since a notice had been received, it had to be replied to. The date fixed was 25.11.2008 at the Lucknow Bench of the Allahabad High Court.

The Additional Secretary (Border Management) advised the Union Home Secretary to depute me to attend the court hearing of this scam. Ahmad had stated that he had supervised my work in the Department of Industrial Policy and Promotion and was aware that I had handled a lot of court cases there. Hence, while the delegation went to Islamabad, I went to Lucknow.

I had got an Affidavit prepared and got it signed by the Home Secretary before his departure, which was filed in the High Court of Allahabad in its Lucknow Bench. The then Assistant Solicitor General, R Dwivedi, attended the court with me and got the complaint discharged on the same day, ie. 25 November 2008. So, I decided to return to Delhi on the same evening.

I was waiting to take the flight back to Delhi at the Lucknow Airport when I received a call from a +92 number. I disconnected. The phone rang again. This time I picked up the call… it was Director (IS) from Islamabad. He said that since the agenda could not be completed, the delegation's stay in Pakistan had been extended by one more day. I was to get the paper formalities completed for the extension the next day.

On 26.11.2008, I had got the stay extension formalities completed and emailed the formal orders to the High Commission of India, Islamabad.

It later came to my knowledge that actually, the delegates were reluctant to extend their stay. But the Additional Secretary (Border Management), who was the senior-most after the Home Secretary in the delegation, advised the Home Secretary in favour of a one-day stay over. Since all other officers were junior to him, no one countered him. The stay got extended on the pretext of a meeting with Interior Minister Rehman Malik on 26.11.2008 afternoon.

The meeting with Rehman Malik is reported to have taken place in the afternoon of 26 November.

Thereafter, the delegation was taken to Murree. Everything about it is already in the public domain. The information has all been obtained by RTI by my media friend Geeta Mohan, then with *NewsX* and now with *India Today* TV. Subsequently, several news channels have telecast the vivid details of how the

Indian security establishment got stuck in Murree when there was a terror attack on in Mumbai. The design of the Pakistani establishment in extending the stay by one day, then taking the delegation to Murree where the communication systems are feeble, became evident.

But was there a mole in the Indian team? We do not know. However, the buildup to the talks can throw some light, especially the inclusion of the Additional Secretary (BM) as a member of the delegation. This was done at the behest of some political command. The said officer was of higher rank than all the other delegates except for the Home Secretary, who was the leader. May I underline that in government working, when two officers have to present different views before the leader, the senior of the two has higher chance of prevailing. This has been borne out by experience in this case.

It was later revealed that two officers in the team, who were Joint Secretaries representing the two intel agencies, had some detailed inputs of a potential attack on India but they could not prevail upon the Secretary vis-à-vis the Additional Secretary about not staying the extra day.

One JS, the person who had more details of inputs on a possible attack returned to Delhi early, citing some urgent work on the morning of 26 November.

It is now clear that the Home Secretary and the leader of delegation had succumbed to bureaucratic hierarchy and listened to his Number Two instead of to the persons with relevant inputs and had put the nation in a quandary. His presence and his team's presence would have enabled a better calibration of response to 26/11 and may be, with lesser casualties and damages. In hindsight, one can also say, for any HSLT, why do all the important people have to be in Pakistan in this age of technology? The entire Home department was in Pakistan during the 1.6.2006 attack on the RSS headquarters in Nagpur, which could have been something big. It was the same on 26/11.

Although we were prepared for a terror attack any time, I never had any premonition of the things to come that evening. Again, there are certain questions that beg for answers.

Why was the Additional Secretary (Border Management), who is conventionally not a member of the Indian delegation, included?

Who lobbied for inclusion of the Additional Secretary in the delegation?

Why did the delegation not stick to the predetermined time schedule?

Why did the leader of delegation not pay heed to his two vital assets, instead of overwhelmingly going by the suggestion of his Number Two?

Was there any hidden agenda in the orchestrations of the Number Two of the delegation?

Night of 26/11 to Afternoon of 27/11

IT WAS COLD on the night of 26.11.2008 in Delhi. Since it was a very light day at work, I left the office somewhat early. It was a mild winter night, and I was reclining on the bed and just surfing the channels on my television set as I knew that my control over the remote would be short-lived. My wife was cleaning up after dinner, she would join me, as was the routine. While surfing the channels (mostly news and sports), I noticed that some law and order disturbance were being reported from Mumbai in some channels. I called up the MHA Control Room to ascertain what was happening. I was informed initially that it was some gang war going on. This was at about 9:00 pm.

Within 15 minutes, I received a call from the Control Room. I was informed by one of the staffers, *'Sahib, Mumbai mein pataka baj gaya'*. There had been terrorist attacks in two hotels and other prominent locations. The entire top management of the Home Ministry dealing with Internal Security was in Pakistan. They had gone there for the Home Secretary-level talks with Pakistan. Farcically, the theme of the talks was *Counter Terrorism and Combating Drug Trafficking.*

Both the themes, in my personal opinion, bespoke of Pakistan's hypocrisy. Firstly, any sensible initiatives proposed/ led by any Indian delegation relating to combating terrorism in the region is always deflected by Pakistan. They find ways and means to not accept the Indian proposals. Also, they suggest such modifications which will render the entire instrument futile.

In the 2007 innings of HSLT, held in Le Meridian Hotel in New Delhi, I had seen this happen and I hold no illusions about the HSLTs. In 2007 in India, Pakistan raised the issue of some Lal Masjid attacks in Islamabad and the Pakistani Secretary (Interior), their leader of the delegation, walked away from the meeting after the first day, rendering the entire second day's proceeding infructuous.

Similar was the predicament of cooperation on combating drug trafficking in the region. A Memorandum of Understanding was to have been signed between the Narcotics Control Bureau of India and the Anti-Narcotics Force of Pakistan. The framework had been finalised in the first HSLT in 2005 and this was the 4th innings and the Pakistan team always came up with some objections or modifications or the other which would have the effect of annulling the entire MOU. These can be corroborated from the Joint Statement issued after the conclusion of every such talk. I would advise readers to access the Joint Statement of 3rd or 4th July 2007.

Having received the message about the terror attacks in Mumbai at about 9:30 pm, I asked the Control Room if my presence would help. I knew well that the MHA Control Room was manned by personnel from the armed forces and the duty officers were generally Deputy or Assistant Commandants. At that juncture, I remember, the duty officer was a CRPF man who was also a very affable guy. I asked him if he could find me transportation to get to the MHA Control Room? He sent a vehicle and I reached the Control Room at about 10:30 pm. Upon reaching the Control Room, I took over the job of obtaining information and assessing the updated status.

I would like to state two things. Firstly, we generally knew with experience, the information that is required to be collected in the event of such attacks. After all, so far 2008 had been one of the bloodiest years for terror attacks in the hinterlands of the country. We had started the year with a terror attack on 1.1.2008 on the CRPF Camp at Rampur.

When I reached the MHA, there was mayhem in the Control Room. Those manning the Control Room were flooded with calls from the PMO, the Ministry of External Affairs, the Cabinet Secretariat, Embassies and all and sundry.

By 11 pm, two joint secretaries had also joined the team. One was the Joint Secretary in charge of Police Deployment and he had spoken to DG, NSG for immediate movement of troops to Mumbai. Another Joint Secretary was handling the dissemination of information to the PMO, Cabinet Secretariat et al. I was relatively undisturbed, focusing on getting the updates from a Senior Inspector in the ATS. This man was Dinesh Agarwal, the only surviving ATS Mumbai staffer, who was my only source of information at that point in time. Hassan Gafoor, Mumbai's Commissioner of Police was reportedly at the Taj Mahal Hotel. His 2nd in command, K L Prasad was at Trident, overseeing the rescue operations there.

Locally-stationed forces

The government had called in the National Security Guards and NSG movement to Mumbai had begun. Minister of Home, Shivraj Patil wanted to accompany the NSG team. He had suggested this and then went incommunicado.

In the meanwhile, from the ATS reports available, we

became aware that the Mumbai ATS had lost a few officers and policemen and the terrorists were still wreaking havoc in both these hotels.

Calls were made to the Home Minister's residence seeking permission to deploy locally-available resources so that the damage could be controlled to whatever extent. But clearance from the Home Minister's residence was not forthcoming.

Other than the NSG, Mumbai itself always has several experienced forces stationed in the city and its periphery. We have the Central Paramilitary Forces in operation in Mumbai. The Central Industrial Security Force, which is a specialised force competent in securing vital installations like these hotels, could have salvaged the situation before the arrival of the NSG. They are deployed at Mumbai Airport, Rashtriya Chemicals and Fertilizers etc. Further, there was a battalion of the CRPF at Navi Mumbai, which could have been moved quickly as immediate reinforcement and some sort of first aid. But with no clearance coming forth from the Home Minister, timely action could not be taken and these specialised forces remained immobile and unused even as terrorists wreaked havoc on the nation's financial hub.

I was in the Home Ministry. *I don't want to comment on the deployment of MARCOS or why an Army Unit from J&K—redeployed in Mumbai very close to the location at that time—was not deployed as they are under the domain of Ministry of Defence, yet the question did cross my mind.*

The NSG team reached the Delhi Airport by about 1:30 am, but the Home Minister was not ready. The entire sequence of events have been well captured by a leading journalist, Sandeep Unnithan, very aptly and accurately in his work. A lot of lives could have been saved but for the lackadaisical attitude of the then Home Minister.

Those in the thick of things knew that damage could have been reduced to a great extent if locally stationed special forces had been immediately deployed, but they were helpless, bound by the tyranny of hierarchy that bureaucracies are plagued with at such times of crisis. The Home Minister appeared unconcerned during the entire episode.

After the NSG landed in Mumbai and events subsequent to that, we kept a close watch on the progress of the counter measures, while at the same time collected information on the casualties of civilian persons, security force personnel etc. so that the same could be included in the brief to be handed over to the Home Secretary as soon as he landed in Delhi.

We were informed that the Home Secretary and his team were expected to land in Delhi at about 3:00 pm on 27.11.2008. We were also told that the Cabinet Secretary had scheduled a meeting which was expected to commence immediately after the Home Secretary landed in Delhi. Hence, he was to report to the Cabinet Secretary's office directly from the airport. One of the Private Secretaries was to go and receive the Home Secretary at the airport to convey the instructions to him from different authorities like the Cabinet Secretary, the PMO etc. I had prepared the paper on the entire sequence of the Mumbai events, as had been obtained from ATS Senior Inspector Agarwal and handed my report over to this Private Secretary, who also happened to be a good friend. I had told him that I was going home as I had been in the North Block since the previous night. Generally, I was known in the MHA as a man with relentless capacity to work, but I must confess, that afternoon I really felt exhausted.

That day, after a much-deserved bath and prayers, I went to sleep early in the evening, knowing fully well that the coming few days would be quite hectic, given the gravity and magnitude of the attacks and also given the fact, Parliament was in session and this incident would trigger a host of Parliament questions, calling attention notices etc.

The porous coastline

Secondly, we had this input about a possible attack through the coastal route and had shared the input with the concerned State governments with coastlines. About a week before the 26/11 attack, the Indian coastal security forces had sighted a ship in Pakistani waters, which had later moved into the margins of the Indian waters, but we could not take any action against this errant vessel. However, the sighting had reaffirmed that any time, an attack through the sea route was possible.

During the course of collection and collation of information about the terrorist attacks, two intriguing facts that I came to know agitated me. They still agitate me.

Firstly, it has been said that the terrorists were dropped a few kilometers from the Colaba coastal area. From there, they swam ashore and then walked through the fishermen's habitation (a *basti*) and entered into Mumbai city from the Badhwar Park.

One has to know the cultural sensitivities of the fishermen community. They do not tolerate any stranger or intruder walking through their colony. Here, we are told to believe that there were ten strange men, all armed to the teeth with some of the most potent arms and ammunitions, and walking through the colony.

It is stupid to believe that they passed through unnoticed. The assumed transit time of these terrorists must have been between 7-7:30 pm in the evening. This is a time when it is almost impossible to go through this colony unnoticed. *Were there people from within the community who helped these strangers pass through the place? If so who were they?* I have my suspicion about one political leader who was at that time wearing the mantle of being leader of this community.

Subsequently, Union Minister A R Antulay's statements in the media generated a lot of debate in Parliament. The extracts of the debate dated 19.12.2008 in the Rajya Sabha, says:

Death of ATS Chief Hemant Karkare in Terrorist Attach In Mumbai

श्री एस. एस. अहलुवालिया (झारखंड): उपसभापति महोदय, अभी 26 तारीख से लेकर 29 तारीख तक मुंबई में जो घटना घटी है, उसको इस सदन में बड़ी गंभीरता से लिया गया, जिसके कारण हमने कल National Investigative Agency Bill और Unlawful Activities (Prevention) Amendment Bill पास किया और सर्वसम्मति से पास किया।

महोदय, जब हम उनको श्रद्धांजलि देते हैं, तो हम लोग गुनगुनाते हैं या बोलते हैं कि "शहीदों की चिताओं पर लगेंगे हर बरस मेले, वतन पर मरने वालों का बाकी यही निशान होगा" और हम अपनी श्रद्धा के सुमन उनके चरणों में चढ़ाते हैं। मुंबई के ताज होटल में जब यह घटना घट रही थी, उसी समय पाकिस्तान के एक चैनल न्यूज वन ने पाकिस्तान में तरह-तरह का कुप्रचार शुरू किया। उसने यह कह कर कुप्रचार शुरू किया कि ये जो दस आदमी हैं, वे पाकिस्तानी नहीं हैं, बल्कि वे हिन्दू आतंकवादी हैं और Raw और IB मिल कर यह सब कर रही है, चूंकि प्रज्ञा सिंह और कर्नल पुरोहित को गिरफ्तार किया गया है, इसलिए यह सारा चक्रांत हो रहा है। यह पूरा प्रोग्राम पाकिस्तान टी.वी. पर दिखाया गया है। मुझे आश्चर्य होता है कि उसने जो बात कही और उसकी बात का जो अक्स है, जो merit है या जो demerit है, जो issue है, उसी बात की जांच, उसी बात की मांग आज केन्द्रीय मंत्रालय का एक मंत्री कर रहा है। पाकिस्तान का जो website है, कल उसने कहा और आज अखबार में headline छपा है कि "Mr. Antulay, why are you helping Pakistan?" यह Mail Today का headline है और ऊपर से कहा गया, "Remarks casting doubts on circumstances of Karkare's death fuel Pak propaganda while opportunists are eying for votes." यह तो है ही और साथ ही यह भी है, "Has Union Minority Affairs Minister played into Pakistan's hands by saying that there is more than what meets the eye, and that Maharashtra ATS Chief, Hemant Karkare, was killed by terrorism plus something?" A big question mark! And, then, Sir, a Pakistani news website has picked up Antulay's statement and said on Thursday, "Antulay seems to have borrowed a leaf from Pakistani TV host who has claimed that Mumbai terrorist attacks were the handiwork of "Hindu Zionists" कि आज जब यह मैसेज, एक केंद्रीय मंत्री अगर पिछले तीन दिन से ...***(समय की घंटी)***... मैं कंप्लीट कर रहा हूं सर। पिछले तीन दिन से वे यह बात उठा रहे हैं तो अभी तक प्रधान मंत्री ने, सरकार ने उनसे यह सवाल क्यों नहीं पूछा? अगर आपको इतना ही विश्वास है उनकी बात पर और उनकी आवाज पर, तो आप इनक्वायरी करा लीजिए। अगर इनक्वायरी नहीं करा रहे हैं, तो पूरे राष्ट्र को भ्रम में डालकर क्यों रख रहे हैं? ...**(व्यवधान)**... और पाकिस्तान का जो tirade चल रहा है भारत के खिलाफ, इसको बल मिल रहा है, इसको शक्ति मिल रही है। तो ये किनके हाथों में खेल रहे हैं? दाऊद इब्राहिम के हाथों में खेल रहे हैं या पाकिस्तानी आई.एस.आई. के हाथों में खेल रहे हैं, यह जानने की जरूरत है और इस पर सख्त कार्यवाही करने की जरूरत है। ये अपनी जबान बंद करें, नहीं तो जनता इनकी जबान बंद करेगी।

श्री मनोहर जोशी (महाराष्ट्र): सर, यह जो विषय अहलुवालिया जी ने उठाया है, बहुत महत्वपूर्ण विषय है, बहुत गंभीर विषय है और इस विषय पर मैं अपने विचार आपके सामने रख रहा हूं।

सर, यह बात तो मैं जानता हूं, पूरी दुनिया जानती है कि तीनों अफसर जो मारे गए करकरे, कामते और सालस्कर - तीनों को आतंकवादियों ने मारा है। जो आतंकवादी पकड़ा गया है, जिसका नाम कसाब है, उसका जवाब भी आया है कि ये हत्याएं उसने की हैं। केवल इतना ही नहीं सर, महाराष्ट्र के गृह मंत्री ने भी निवेदन किया है और वह निवेदन यही है कि हत्या करने वाले आतंकवादी हैं। इतनी बात होने पर भी मुझे बड़ा अचरज लगता है कि महाराष्ट्र से आने वाले एक मंत्री ए.आर. अंतुले क्यों कहते हैं कि ऐसा नहीं हुआ है, दूसरी कुछ बात इसके पीछे है!

यानी लोगों के मन में संशय का निर्माण करना क्या ठीक है? और जो पाकिस्तान की भूमिका है, वही भूमिका जब भारत सरकार के एक मंत्री उठाते हैं, तो मैं नहीं समझता हूं कि उन्हें मंत्रिमंडल में रहने की कोई जरूरत है। इसलिए हम चाहते हैं कि इस विषय को छोड़ना नहीं चाहिए। यह विषय लोक सभा में भी उठा और बाहर भी उठा, हर न्यूजपेपर ने निवेदन किया कि ऐसे मंत्री को निकालने की आवश्यकता है, लेकिन यह बात होने के बावजूद अंतुले जी कहते हैं कि मैंने जो कहा, वह ठीक है और मैं यह नहीं समझता हूं कि उनकी पार्टी अभी तक उनके विरुद्ध कुछ कार्यवाही क्यों नहीं करती है? मैं यह मानने को तैयार नहीं हूं कि जो मंत्री ऐसी भूमिका लेगा कि जो भूमिका पाकिस्तान को मंजूर है, ऐसी भूमिका लेने वाले मंत्री को केवल इस्तीफा देकर नहीं, उनको गवर्नमेंट के मंत्रिमंडल से निकालना चाहिए और यही हमारी मांग है, इसलिए मैं यहां खड़ा हुआ हूं। मैं चाहता हूं कि इस विषय को छोड़ना नहीं चाहिए। सभी लोगों ने एकमत से यहां एक प्रस्ताव मंजूर किया, वैसे ही एकमत से लोगों को कहना चाहिए कि जो आदमी देश के खिलाफ बोलता है, उसको मंत्रिमंडल में रहने का कोई भी अधिकार नहीं। ...(**व्यवधान**)...

श्री साबिर अली (बिहार): उपसभापति महोदय, ...(**व्यवधान**)...

MR. DEPUTY CHAIRMAN: No, no. ...*(Interruptions)*... There is no notice. In Zero Hour, nobody is allowed in this manner. *(Interruptions)* Please. Let us observe the ...*(Interruptions)*... There are other members also. ...*(Interruptions)*...

श्री मनोहर जोशी: इसलिए मैं चाहता हूं कि तुरंत इस विषय पर कार्यवाही हो और यदि गवर्नमेंट इस विषय पर कुछ कार्यवाही करने को तैयार नहीं है, तो मैं नहीं सोचता हूं कि हम गवर्नमेंट का निषेध करने के बगैर रह सकते हैं, हमें भी गवर्नमेंट का निषेध करना पड़ेगा। ...*(समय की घंटी)*... मेरी प्रार्थना है कि अंतुले जी का इस्तीफा तुरंत लेने की आवश्यकता है।

श्री उपसभापति: श्री भारतकुमार राऊत, बोलिए। ...(**व्यवधान**)...

श्री एस.एस. अहलुवालिया: सर, संविधान के अनुसार ...(**व्यवधान**)...

MR. DEPUTY CHAIRMAN: I have called Mr. Raut ...*(Interruptions)*... No, no. Please. ...*(Interruptions)*... Mr. Raut, please speak. ...*(Interruptions)*... Please don't ask for time. ...*(Interruptions)*... आप बैठिए। Nothing will go on record except what Mr. Raut says. ...*(Interruptions)*... आप बैठिए ...(**व्यवधान**)... Mr. Raut, please start. ...*(Interruptions)*... आप बैठिए।

श्री साबिर अली: *

श्री एस.एस. अहलुवालिया: *

MR. DEPUTY CHAIRMAN: Please आप बैठिए। Nothing will go on record except what Mr. Raut says. ...*(Interruptions)*... साबिर अली जी, आपको लिखकर देना चाहिए था बोलने के लिए।

SHRI BHARATKUMAR RAUT (Maharashtra): Sir, I stand here to support the feelings expressed by hon. Member, Shri Ahluwaliay ji and, my leader, Shri Manohar Joshi ji.

Sir, I wish to express the deep anguish and anger of the people of Maharashtra, in particular, and, the people of India, in general.

Sir, he is a Minister of the Union Cabinet who has been entrusted with the responsibility of running the Government and running the nation. Is he a Minister of the Indian Government, or, **

MR. DEPUTY CHAIRMAN: Please remove these words from record.

*Not recorded.

** Exoybged as ordered by the Chair.

SHRI BHARATKUMAR RAUT: Sir, I make a statement that this is because he has been playing in the hands of Pakistan.

श्री उपसभापति: 'Minister of Pakistan' निकाल दीजिए।

SHRI BHARATKUMAR RAUT: Sir, it is not an abrupt statement. ...*(Interruptions)*...

MR. DEPUTY CHAIRMAN: Please remove it. ...*(Interruptions)*...

SHRI BHARATKUMAR RAUT: It seems that ...*(Interruptions)*...

MR. DEPUTY CHAIRMAN: That is different. ...*(Interruptions)*... That is different. ...*(Interruptions)*... You can't call him a Minister of Pakistan. ...*(Interruptions)*... आप बैठिए। वे बोल रहे हैं। ...(**व्यवधान**)... कुछ रिकॉर्ड में नहीं जाएगा।

SHRI BHARATKUMAR RAUT: Sir, the incident happened ...*(Interruptions)*... The incident happened on 26th and Mr. Antulay raised the issue on 17th. So, what was he doing for 21 days? Why did he choose this time? He chose this time very meticulously, with the great design, when the House, the Lok Sabha, was discussing the NIA Bill and the Unlawful Activities Prevention Bill. At that time, outside the House, he raised this issue. If he wanted to have a sincere effort, he could have raised this issue within the House, as a Member of the House. Why did he choose to go out of the House, called the television channels and raised the issue there? It is a design to create an atmosphere of suspicion; it is a design to disturb the fabric of socio-religious harmony and unity of this country. Sir, I make a statement that it is the responsibility of the Prime Minister now ...*(Interruptions)*... It is the responsibility of the Prime Minister now first to take apology from him and then sack him from the Ministry. Both things are equally important. First he should be apologised because then only the Government can say that it is not party to it. After that he should be sacked. ...*(Interruptions)*...

SHRI MANOHAR JOSHI: Sir, the Government should respond on it.

MR. DEPUTY CHAIRMAN: I can't force the Government to response.

SHRI BHARATKUMAR RAUT; In this connection, let me again tell you that if the Government ...*(Interruptions)*...

MR. DEPUTY CHAIRMAN: Please. ...*(Interruptions)*... Please, Mr. Jethmalani, I request you ...*(Interruptions)*... Because during Zero Hour, if I allow you to speak, I will have to allow every one. ...*(Interruptions)*...

SHRI BHARATKUMAR RAUT: Lok Sabha should have some instrument by which Antulay is impeached. We should impeach him if the Government fails to sack him. *(Time-bell rings)* That is the feeling of the people in general. Thank you. ...*(Interruptions)*...

MR. DEPUTY CHAIRMAN: Zero Hour is over. ...*(Interruptions)*... We will now take up the Science and Engineering Research Board Bill, 2008.

...*(Interruptions)*...

Re. Statement by Government

THE MINISTER OF STATE IN THE MINISTRY OF PARLIAMENTARY AFFAIRS AND THE MINISTER OF STATE IN THE MINISTRY OF PLANNING (SHRI V. NARAYANSAMY): Mr. Deputy Chairman, Sir, I would like to respond. ...*(Interruptions)*...

MR. DEPUTY CHAIRMAN: I think, the Government is responding. ...*(Interruptions)*...

SHRI V. NARAYANASAMY: I would like to respond, Sir. ...*(Interruptions)*...

MR. DEPUTY CHAIRMAN: Mr. Narayanasamy wants to respond. ...*(Interruptions)*... The Minister wants to respond.

श्री रामदास अग्रवाल (राजस्थान): सर, ...(**व्यवधान**)...

श्री उपसभापति: आप बैठिए। वे बोल रहे हैं। ...(**व्यवधान**)... कुछ रिकॉर्ड में नहीं जाएगा। ...*(Interruptions)*... Nothing will go on record. ...(Interruptions).. Mr. Sabir Ali, please sit down. ...*(Interruptions)*... Nothing will go on record. ...*(Interruptions)*... आप बैठिए। ...(**व्यवधान**)... साबिर अली जी, मैं कह रहा हूं कि आप प्लीज़ बैठ जाइए। ...(**व्यवधान**)...

SHRI V. NARAYANASAMY: Hon. Deputy Chairman, Sir, the hon. Members have expressed their feelings in the august House. The hon. Minister for External Affairs has already mentioned in the Lok Sabha that the Government will respond on the issue that the hon. Members have raised as regards our senior Cabinet colleague Shri Antulayji. The Government's response will definitely be coming to this House also. ...*(Interruptions)*... Kindly have some patience. ...*(Interruptions)*... We will tell you. We are going to sit up to 23rd of this month. Therefore, the Government will definitely come forward and explain the position. ...*(Interruptions)*...

SHRI MANOHAR JOSHI (Maharashtra): I need your ...*(Interruptions)*...

MR. DEPUTY CHAIRMAN: Mr. Manohar Joshi ji, the Government have assured to come out with a statement. That is sufficient. ...*(Interruptions)*... We will now take up the Science and Engineering Research Board Bill, 2008. Mr. Kapil Sibal. ...*(Interruptions)*...

Now I will briefly explain the relationship between Parliament and government in respect of furnishing of information. A Member of Parliament has every right to ask for information available with the government and its policies and proposed steps etc. This can be done through several enabling Rules framed by both Houses of Parliament which provides for instruments like Starred Questions for oral answers, Unstarred Questions for written answers, Short Notice Questions, Half-an-hour discussions, Calling the Attention of the Government etc.

If, during the relevant allotted time of discussion, the information sought by the Member cannot be fully provided, the replying Minister makes a promise on behalf of the government, which is known as an 'assurance'. The statement of deputy minister V Narayanaswamy, who was replying on behalf of the Minister, as you have read, became an assurance. Since the domain was that of the Ministry of Home Affairs, we had to fulfil this promise. You can sense how challenging it must have been to fulfil this promise.

The second fact in my knowledge that agitates me even ten years since the incident is that the Additional Chief Secretary (Home), Chitkala Zutshi of the Government of Maharashtra, was present within the Taj Hotel when the attack began.

I remember Peter, the CRPF Commandant manning the Control Room, asking me in jest if this officer had gone to Taj to inaugurate the attack. This was as soon as we came to know that this officer was present there at the time of the attack.

According to the information we received, Zutshi was escorted out of Taj Mahal Hotel even while the attack was in progress, without even a scratch. This officer must have been one of the few persons who got out of the Taj Mahal Hotel after the attacks began. In an interview to *Mumbai Mirror*, in 2009, Zutshi said that her presence at the Taj Mahal Hotel was to attend a *personal* dinner.

Normally there is a joke that *bureaucrats ke jeb se paisa nahi nikalta* (meaning, money doesn't come out of a bureaucrat's pocket). This includes me. At the same time, one must remember that both, the CCS Conduct Rules applicable to central services and corresponding provision under the All-India Services, do permit that a casual meal etc. can be accepted as a gift. Hence, there is no violation of the Conduct Rules involved here.

To clear the air of suspicion, Additional Chief Secretary Zutshi could have come clean by revealing the name of the host who was with her in the hotel. If the bureaucrat herself was the host, it would have been appropriate for her to reveal who she was hosting that evening. This would have helped clear the air of suspicion around her presence at the Taj that evening when the most horrendous carnage was perpetrated on the city of Mumbai. Excerpts of her interview:

> Additional Chief Secretary (Home), Chitkala Zutshi: I was at the Taj with friends for dinner when we heard gunshots around 9:35 pm. We realised it was a terrorist attack. Luckily, the terrorists didn't come to where we were on the first floor. For seven hours, we were stuck there. I made several calls to policemen and officials I knew. I also had an additional responsibility because of my job. Around 4:30 am, the firemen finally rescued us.

In the book, *The Siege - Attack on Taj*, Adrian Levy and Cathy Scott Clarke have captured the entire events that happened at the Taj Hotel on that night. It is evident from their well-researched work, in which they closely interviewed the survivors including the Managers and other employees of Taj Mahal Hotel, no one was reported to have escaped once the terrorist took charge of the hotel till they were rescued by the NSG. This included powerful bankers, influential businessmen etc. *How come that Zutshi's escape does not find a mention anywhere? And not one of the 'friends' with her, who also presumably escaped with her, have so far spoken up.*

Importantly, the person who escaped was a senior serving bureaucrat of the State government discharging responsibility inter alia of securing the same places which were penetrated by terrorists. They came from the same route about which this officer had inputs from the Union government. Still the officer was present, as per her own admission, at the attack site with 'friends' safely, and escaped unharmed.

What is intriguing about this officer's presence is that inputs about such attacks had always been shared with the Chief Secretary/DGP and Home Department of the government of Maharashtra. This officer was privy to all such inputs. According to the laid-down procedure, the input/s after perusal by the Chief Secretary lands straight on the desk of the Additional Chief Secretary of the domain concerned. Zutshi was the concerned domain officer. Hence the officer could not have been oblivious to the inputs and the potential threat. To me personally, the presence of the officer and her subsequent escape unscathed does not appear a mere coincidence.

More importantly, I will recall the transcripts of certain calls between the handlers and the perpetrators of the attack at the Mumbai Taj. This conversation has been included in the dossier submitted to Pakistan. There is a reference to three Cabinet Ministers and one Secretary in the transcripts. The handler states that 'they are assets'.

> Greetings! There are three Ministers and one Secretary of the Cabinet in your hotel. We don't know in which room.
> Oh! That is good news. It is the icing on the cake.
> Find those 3-4 persons and then get whatever you want from India.

Under the circumstances, how is it that this Additional Chief Secretary (Zutshi) was left unscathed in the attack?

The terrorists came via the sea route and reached Colaba. Thereafter, they walked through the fishermen's colony, came over to Badhwar Park. Thereafter, they travelled around Mumbai as if they had been living in the city for ages. Even after a decade, it all sounds like a fairy tale.

I for one, from day one, have been of the view that these intruders could not have walked through the fishermen's colony or travelled from Badhwar Park to their respective locations without local support. Local support with so much of inputs (like who were present inside the Taj Hotel) being available at the highest level, this support could not have been without backing of any institutional-level mechanism or without some strong political or powerful group's backing.

When the situation had been brought under control, the then Chief Minister of Maharashtra, Vilasrao Deshmukh, made a customary visit to the locations, within a few days of the incidents. He was accompanied by film producers. *Was he trying to sell this as a film plot is a question that often crops up. If so, had the political establishment partnered the perpetrators and their supporters is another questions that begs an answer.*

These are questions which have agitated me not only because of the certain unfortunate experiences I underwent in the days following the attacks and the revelations after the incidents, but also because of several other sequences of events. Suffice it to say that any one joining the dots cannot rule out the possibility and infer that many members of the governments of the day or persons having the blessings of the respective governments had partnered, harboured and covered up for the perpetrators. This is a strong statement but I have seen the records, been privy to many discussions, formal and informal, and so such an inference is being drawn.

Beyond this, to get to the level of confirmation may involve sharing of information about operational instruments. However, once again, I am recalling the Dossier on Mumbai Terror Attack which was handed over to Pakistan by the Indian Foreign Office in January 2009.[8]

A January 2009 English language report on the attacks dossier, produced by the Indian Ministry of External Affairs

---

8 https://archive.org/stream/MumbaiTerrorAttacksDossier/MumbaiTerrorAttacksDossier_djvu.txt.
http://www.paperlessarchives.com/free_titles.h

with the assistance of the FBI, reads:

> *A January 2009 English language report*
> The 2008 Mumbai attacks were more than ten coordinated shooting and bombing attacks across Mumbai, India's largest city on November 26, 2008 and lasted until November 29, 2008, killing at least 173 people and wounding at least 308. Eight of the attacks occurred in South Mumbai: at Chhatrapati Shivaji Terminus, the Oberoi Trident, the Taj Mahal Palace & Tower, Leopold Cafe, Cama Hospital, the Nariman House, the Metro Cinema, and a lane behind the Times of India building and St. Xavier's College. There was also an explosion at Mazagaon, in Mumbai's port area, and in a taxi at Vile Parle.
>
> —*This can be found in Annexure-I of the Indo-Pak Dossier.*

Terrorist attack on Mumbai (November 26-29, 2008)

1. Mumbai, the commercial capital of India, came under a heinous terrorist attack on November 26, 2008.

2. The terrorist attacks took place at many locations, especially at CST Railway Station; the Leopold Cafe; Taj Hotel; Oberoi Trident Hotel; and Nariman House. 165 persons (civilians and security personnel) lost their lives and 304 were injured. Among the civilians killed were 26 foreigners belonging to many nationalities.

3. Cases have been registered and the investigations have been entrusted to the Crime Branch of the Mumbai Police.

4. The investigations have revealed that ten terrorists were involved in the attacks. Nine were killed in the operations; one was captured alive. His name is Mohammed Ajmal Amir Kasab. He has been arrested.

5. The following facts have been put together based on the interrogation of the captured/arrested terrorist and other

evidence gathered so far.

Mohammad Ajmal Amir Kasab

6. He is the son of Mohammed Amir Kasab resident of Village Faridkot, District Okara in the Province of Punjab in Pakistan. He has stated that along with many others, including the nine terrorists who were killed, he was trained at Laskhar-e-Taiba training camps located at Muridke, Manshera and Muzaffarabad.

7. Initially, the group consisted of 32 persons. They were imparted (training) of firearms, ammunition, grenades and explosives. Later, they were taught to handle and fire Kalashnikov rifles and 9mm pistols and also how to fabricate explosive devices. They were also imparted training in techniques to counter interrogation and tolerate pain,they were indoctrinated to become suicide attackers.

8. Ultimately, 13 persons out of the group were selected for the attacks in India. Six of the 13 were sent for some (operations in) Kashmir. Three new members were brought into the group, making the number 10. One of the new members was Ismail Khan who, eventually, became the leader of the group. The 10-member group was told about the Mumbai operations in mid-September 2008. At this point, the 10 members of the group were kept in isolation in a house near Karachi and all contact between the group and others were cut off.

9. The group was closely monitored by Zaki-Ur-Rehman Lakhvi, Abu Hamza Yousuf alias Muzammil and Kaahfa, all senior functionaries of the LeT. The first three are known to intelligence agencies of many countries.

10. Mohammed Ajmal Amir Kasab has disclosed the names and identities of the other nine terrorists who were killed in the operations.

(i) Ismail Khan (25 yrs) r/o Dera Ismail Khan, NWFP, Pakistan

(ii) Babar Imran @ Abu Akasha (25 yrs) r/o Multan, Pakistan

(iii) Naser @ Abu Umar (23 yrs) r/o Faisalabad, Pakistan

(iv) Shoaib @ Abu Saheb (21 yrs) r/o Shakkargarh Naroval, Sialkoat, Pakistan

(v) Nazir @ Abu Umer (28 yrs) r/o Faisalabad, Pakistan

(vi) Hafiz Arshad @ Abu Abdar Rehman (Bada - 23 yrs)

(vii) Javed @ Abu AM (22 yrs) r/o Okara, Pakistan

(viii) Abdur Rehman @ Abu Abdar Rehman (Chhota - 21 yrs) r/o Arifwala, Multan Road, Pakistan

(ix) Fahadulla (23 yrs) r/o Ujrashah Mukim, Rasur Road, Okara,Punjab, Pakistan.

11. On the basis of the interrogation and searches, the investigators have recovered the following material objects:

(i) M.V. Kuber, a fishing trawler

(ii) GPS instruments

(iii) A satellite phone

(iv) An eleven seater inflatable dinghy with outboard motor

(v) Numerous articles (list with photographs at Annexure-II)

MV Kuber was a fishing trawler that belonged to Vinod Bhai Masani of Porbander in the State of Gujarat, India. As the narration below will show, the vessel was hijacked by the terrorist group.

> The eleven-seater inflatable dinghy was recovered off the shore near Badhwar Park, Mumbai. It was fitted with an outboard motor made by Yamaha Motor Corporation. An attempt was made by the terrorists to erase the engine number but it has been retrieved by the investigators.
>
> The outboard motor number is 67 CL-1020015 manufactured by Yamaha Motor Corporation, Japan and imported into Pakistan and distributed by a company by name 'Business & Engineering Trends' located at No. 24, Habibullah Road, off Davis Road, Lahore. The telephone number of the company is +92 42 63 11044.

The articles that were recovered include toiletries, medical kit, food articles, drums containing diesel, clothing items etc. and they bear clear evidence of having been manufactured in Pakistan. (See in Annexure-II of Indo-Pak Dossier.)

> The terrorists started in a small boat from Karachi at approximately 0800 hrs on 22 November 2008. After traveling for about 40 minutes, they were shifted to a larger boat, 'Al-Husseini', which, according to the captured terrorist, belongs to Zaki-ur-Rehman Lakhvi, Chief Commander of the LeT. There were already seven LeT members on board. The terrorists spent the entire day on board the Af-Husseini. On 23 November, at about 1500 hours, the captured terrorist noticed another boat that docked next to the Al-Husseini. This was an Indian registered fishing vessel called MV Kuber, which had five crew members. Four crew members of MV Kuber were shifted to the Al-Husseini. These four crew members were later killed by the LeT members. The captain of the trawler (Amar Singh Solanki) was allowed to remain on board the MV Kuber and it was he who navigated the MV Kuber for approximately 550 NM to Mumbai.
>
> The ten terrorists were given their individual pack bags, containing a Kalashnikov, ammunition, 9 mm pistols, hand grenades, dry fruits, etc.
>
> They were also handed over a bag each, which contained an IED.

The ten terrorists performed watch duties on board MV Kuber. Logsheets maintained by them have been seized.

(See in Annexure-V of Indo-Pak Dossier.)

The MV Kuber reached a point four nautical miles off Mumbai at 1600 hours on November 26, 2008. As soon as it was dark, the team leader, Ismail Khan, contacted their handler in Pakistan, who directed them to kill Amar Singh Solanki, the captain of MV Kuber. After killing Solanki, the terrorists, along with their weapons and IEDs, boarded the inflatable dinghy. They traversed the last four nautical miles to Mumbai in about 1 hour and 15 minutes, reaching the locality of Badhwar Park (Cuffe Parade) in South Mumbai at about 2030 hours.

After alighting, the ten terrorists divided into five teams according to the pairing decided earlier. Mohammed Ajmal Amir Kasab was paired with the group leader, Ismail Khan. They took taxis to different target destinations. IED devices were planted in two taxis and they later exploded - one at Wadi Bunder and the other at Vile Parle - killing the two taxi drivers.

The target: CST Railway Station

CST Railway Station is the headquarters of Central Railways. More than 3.5 million passengers pass through the station everyday.

At about 21:20 hrs, two terrorists (Mohammed Ajmal Amir Kasab and Ismail Khan) entered the station and started firing indiscriminately from their Kalashnikov rifles and also lobbed grenades. The carnage resulted in 58 dead and 104 injured. They were challenged by a small number of policemen at the station. They left the station, crossed an over-bridge and fled into a lane towards Cama Hospital. Near Cama Hospital they were challenged by a police team and there was an exchange of fire. As they exited the lane, they fired on a police vehicle carrying three senior police officers and four policemen. However, only six were killed and one policeman survived the assault. He is Constable Arun Jadhav and is an eyewitness to the events. After traveling some distance, the terrorists abandoned the police vehicle and hijacked another passenger car. The car came up against a police post where Ismail Khan was killed and Mohammed Ajmal Amir Kasab was captured. An Assistant Sub-Inspector, Tukaram Omble, was killed while overpowering Mohammed Ajmal Amir Kasab. Two police officers were injured.

Police recovered two Kalashnikov rifles, eight magazines, two pistols, ammunition, empty cases and five hand grenades from the two terrorists.

Second Target : Leopold Cafe and Bar

The Leopold Cafe and Bar, established in 1871, is a popular watering hole and is frequented by foreigners as well as Indians.

At about 21:40 hrs, two terrorists {Hafiz Arshad @ Abdul Rehman Bada and Naser @ Abu Umar} entered the Cafe and started firing indiscriminately, using AK-47 assault rifles. One grenade was lobbed and it exploded. Ten persons were killed and many injured. After about five minutes, the two terrorists ran towards the Taj Mahal Hotel, situated about half a kilometer from the Cafe.

Police later recovered from the scene of the attack five AK-47 magazines (of which three were empty and two contained 13 bullets), empty cases of ammunition, one metal butt of an AK-47 rifle and two mobile phones.

Third Target: Taj Mahal Hotel

The Taj Mahal Hotel, constructed in 1903, is a heritage building and an icon in Mumbai. It has two wings, the heritage wing with 290 rooms and the Taj Towers with 275 rooms.

Four terrorists (Shoaib and Javed and the two terrorists who attacked the Leopold Cafe and Bar, namely, Hafiz Arshad and Nasir) targeted the Taj Mahal Hotel. The first pair entered the main lobby at 1:38 hrs and opened fire, killing 20 persons in the first few minutes. The second pair entered the hotel from the North Court entrance at 21:43 hrs and

> fired indiscriminately and hurled grenades. The four terrorists moved up to the sixth floor of the Heritage Wing, killing anyone who came in their way. They set fire to a portion of the hotel. The first, fifth and sixth floors of Heritage Wing were badly gutted.

Some of these events have been captured in the CCTV cameras installed in the hotel.

Eight police personnel from the local police station rushed to the hotel and cordoned off the area. Thereafter, commandos of the Indian Navy reached the hotel. The next morning, the National Security Guards flew in from Delhi and took charge of the operations.

There was a hostage situation because many guests had locked themselves in their rooms and many were sequestered in different parts of the hotel. The operations continued until the morning of 29 November 2008. Nearly 450 guests were rescued. The terrorists killed 32 persons including hotel guests and staff. A Major of the NSG, Sandeep Unnikrishnan, was killed and another commando was injured. At the end of the operations, four terrorists were killed.

> The police recovered four Kalashnikov assault rifles, eight magazines, three pistols and magazines, a number of unexploded grenades, live and empty cases of ammunition, mobile telephones and one GPS instrument.

Throughout the period, the terrorists were in touch with their controllers in Pakistan via telephone. They received a stream of instructions and it was apparent that the controllers were monitoring Indian television channels. The controllers were keen that the terrorists should take hostage some *wazir*s (meaning Ministers) who might have been present in the hotel.

Fourth Target: The Oberoi-Trident Hotel

The hotel has two wings, one named Oberoi and the other Trident.

Together they have 877 rooms. At about 22:00 hrs, two terrorists (Abdul Rehman Chotta and Fahadullah) entered Trident Hotel through the main entrance and started firing indiscriminately. They crossed over to the Oberoi and sprayed bullets into a restaurant. Two IEDs were exploded. The terrorists moved to the upper floors of the Oberoi, killing guests and staff who came in their way. Finally, they holed up on the 16th and 18th floors, where they kept many guests hostage.

NSG Commandos took charge of the operations on the morning of November 27, 2008. The operations were concluded after 42 hours on the afternoon of November 28, 2008. The two terrorists were killed.

In the attack on the Oberoi-Trident, 33 persons were killed. Police recovered two Kalashnikov rifle, six magazines of which two were loaded, a number of empty cases and hand grenade clips.

Fifth Target: Nariman House

Nariman House is a five-storied building, which had been purchased two years ago by an orthodox Jewish organisation called Chabad Liberation Movement of Hasidic Jews. It was renamed as Chabad House. A Rabbi and his family lived in the building and generally accommodated visiting Jews.

At about 22:25 hrs, two terrorists (Babar Imran and Nazir) began firing outside Chabad House and gained access to the building. Several persons were taken hostage. The terrorists and the police exchanged fire throughout the night of November 26, 2008 and into the next day. A powerful IED explosion blew away the wall at the rear of Nariman House. During the operations, the police rescued 14 persons from Chabad House. The maidservant of the Rabbi also escaped, carrying the Rabbi's two-year-old son. The NSG pressed helicopters into service and landed commandos on the terrace of Chabad House. Eventually, both the terrorists were killed.

One NSG Commando was killed and two injured. Five hostages

> were found dead.
>
> Throughout the operations, the terrorists received instructions over telephone from their controllers. The controllers warned the terrorists about the use of helicopters and about the landing of commandos on the terrace.
>
> The police recovered two Kalashnikov rifles, four magazines, three pistols, about 250 live rounds of ammunition, four mobile phones.

Reference has been made to the Kalashnikov rifles, pistols, ammunition, grenades, mobile. Of the ten IED devices that were given to the terrorists, seven had exploded and three were recovered and defused later. The three devices were similar and bear the unmistakable signature of having been made by the same individual or the same team at the same time.

The evidence gathered so far:

> Each IED weighed approximately 8 kilograms and each contained 4-5 kilograms of tightly-packed black greasy RDX. Each had a black-coloured programmable electronic timer switch, with five wires numbered from 1 to 5. Wire numbers 1 and 4 were found connected in all the devices while wire numbers 2, 3 and 5 were left unconnected. Each device had two detonators and steel ball bearings of 4 to 6 mm diameter, which were embedded and placed around the charge. The power source was two 9-volt batteries of Duracell make. The timer bore instructions in Urdu language for setting the time.

The 9 mm pistols that were recovered from different scenes of the crimes bore the marking of the 'Diamond Nedi Frontier Arms Company'.

The hand grenades that were detonated and that were found unexploded were manufactured by Arges, an Austrian company. Inquiries have revealed that Arges Company had given a franchise to manufacture hand grenades to a Pakistan Ordnance Factory near Rawalpindi. Similar hand grenades were used in the serial blasts that shook Mumbai on 12 March 1993 and in the attack on the Parliament House on 13 December 2001. (Photographs of pistols/grenades are in Annexure-VI of Indo-Pak Dossier.)

An email claiming responsibility for the Mumbai attack was sent to the media by a hitherto unknown organisation calling itself 'Deccan Mujahideen'. The IP address of the email ID 'deccanmujahideen@gmail.com' connected to a proxy server in Russia. Examination of the server data has indicated that Zarrar Shah, Communication Coordinator of LeT, had organised the creation of a new email account on the evening of 26 November 2008, specifically in order to send the email claiming responsibility for the attack. It has also been learnt that Zarrar Shah was using another email ID, 'drmoazam@ ymail.com' which was registered from Pakistan via IP address 118,107.140.139 at 1440 Z on 24 June.

The controllers/handlers of the terrorists passed instructions over telephone throughout the operations. They used VOIP calling platforms.

Telephone links

> Investigations into the numbers used by the controllers/ handlers have revealed that one number is a 'Virtual number' and five are DID numbers with the country code of Austria. The virtual number carries the US country code and is +1 201 2531824. This virtual number was used to route calls to the terrorists in India. The virtual number was initially set up with a US company, by name Callphonex, by an individual who identified himself as Kharak Singh from India. The account was activated and transferred in the name of Mohammed Ashfaq.
>
> Kharak Singh also requested Callphonex to assign five Austrian Direct Inward Dialing (DID) numbers because his clients called from different countries, including India. The payment for the account was through Western Union transfer.

> The payment was made to the Western Union agent, Nizar Aisharif whose address is Madina Trading, Corso Garibaldi S3 A, Brescia, BS 25100, Italy with the information: MTCN: 0579326626, Sender: Javaid Iqbal, Amount: US$238.78' on November 25, 2008.

According to Western Union, Javaid Iqbal's date of birth is 31 December 1962 and the Form IV (service provider's ID form that clients fill) he provided was Pakistani. When the phone service provider asked Kharak Singh if he was from India, why did the Western Union transfer come from Pakistan, apparently, Callphonex received no reply. Incidentally, Brigadier Javed Iqbal Cheema was one officer of the ISI well known to people in the Indian intelligence and security establishment at that time. He was a part of the Pakistani delegation for the Home Secretary Level Talks held in New Delhi in July 2007. The question is, was it the same person transferring money through Western Union? I remember him interrupting the Interior Secretary of Pakistan's opening remarks (Syed Kamal Shah) during these talks to put forth the position as desired by his organisation.

Even while the terrorists had occupied the target buildings and the security forces were engaging them, the terrorists were in contact with their controllers/handlers over mobile telephones. They also used mobile telephones belonging to hostages/victims.

Shortly after the attack on Taj Mahal Hotel, Indian agencies were able to intercept mobile telephone calls made from and to the hotel. The controllers/handlers used the virtual number to contact a mobile telephone with one of the terrorists. This conversation was intercepted and, thereafter, all calls made through the virtual number were also intercepted and recorded. The interceptions revealed three Austrian numbers, which were given to the terrorists by the controllers/handlers and conversations with these numbers by the terrorists were also intercepted and recorded. The Austrian numbers correspond to the DID numbers referred to as seen from the records. A sample of the transcripts of the intercepted conversations is in Annexure-VII of the Indo-Pak Dossier. The transcripts show that the terrorists were being instructed and guided by their controllers/handlers.

The interrogation of the captured terrorist revealed a wealth of information. Mohammed Ajmal Amir Kasab claimed that he had met some important LeT leaders. When shown a photograph taken from the passport of the person concerned, he identified the person as the one who had briefed the terrorists in the LeT camps near Muzaffarabad and in Azizabad. He described the person as the most important person in the LeT and the mastermind behind the operations in Mumbai. The photograph shown to him was that of Zaki-ur-Rehman Lakhvi.

The evidence gathered so far unmistakably pointed to the territory of Pakistan as a source of the terrorist attacks in Mumbai between 26-29 November 2008. It is also abundantly clear that senior functionaries of the LeT were the controllers/handlers of the ten terrorists. The evidence unmistakably established that the ten terrorists were chosen, trained, despatched, controlled and guided by the LeT which is the organisation responsible for the attack.

Intercepts of telephonic conversations:[9]
A O A KIA HAL HY.
GUR LGA KNHI.
HUM KHETI BNDR PR HEIN.
SAAD
352384000236350
8821655526412
23.11.08
09:06

9 Audio-transcripts transferred to text form

'MUJH SY IS NUMBER
PER RABTA RAKHNA
HY. WASI'

Log of Kuber
24 hours Poori Safar (24 hours' Complete Journey)
Machli lag rahi hai (Fish is being caught)
Haalat theek hain (Things are OK)
Bhai log (brothers)
Civil Boat
Yaar log (friends)
Navy Boat
Yaar logon ka group (friends'group)
Navy Ship
Machine
Uljhan (problem)
Maal (goods)
Madad (help)
Baraf (Ice)
Safar (journey)
'GR dene wala (3) jama karega aur lene wala khud (3) nakki karega' (GR providers (3) will deposit and receivers (3) themselves will finalise)
Satellite khula rakha hai (10pm - 10am)
(Satellite is on (10pm - 10am)

These are excerpts from Annexure V of the Indo-Pak Dossier
1. Yahan ka phone number (Phone number of this place)
2. Yahan ka satellite number (Satellite number of this place)
3. Naksha ki photographian (Photocopies of maps)
4. Hoyal seton ki simen (SIMs of Hoyal sets)
5. TT pistol 2 (2 TT pistols)
6. Mineral Water Aqua fina
7. Khajoor Achhi 10 kg (good quality dates 10 kg)
8. Current Store Charger
9. GPS ya Navigator (GPS or Navigator)
10. Satellite + phone card

The dinghy list:
1. Biscuit (Candy + bakery)
2. Suiyan (bareek) (thin needles)
3. Aata lal (red flour)
4. Drum (saman ke liye mai tala) (drum with lock to keep things)

Gun 1 piece
Magazine 8 pieces
Grenade 8 pieces
GPS group 1 piece
Chain 1 piece
Itkafi bullets as per requirement
Mobile + Batteries
23270972879217
Colaba, Cuffe Parade, Machlimar Nagar, Raja Bhai Tower, Regal Chowk, Nathalal Marg, Nariman Point, WTC, Regal Cinema
18.56_200

This list is from Annexure V of Indo Pak Dossier
18-56-000
72-67-560
18-55-600
72-48-900
18-5500-300
72-49-56
18-55-190
72-49-500
18-55-180
72-49-535
21° 55’ 470”
68° 17’ 070”
20° 13’ 460”
70° 16’ 370”
18° 56’ 200”
12° 44’ 260”
18° 55’ 100”

72° 49' 310"
72-47-000
75-47-00
23-20---
36----

Names of terrorists figuring in the conversations during the attack (phonetic)

a. *Hotel Taj*
   i) Shuaib
   ii) Ali
   iii) Abdur Rehman
   iv) Umer
   v) Ismail (not present at Taj, killed at Girgaum Choupati)

b. Hotel Trident
   i) Abdul Rehman @ Saquib
   ii) Fahadullah @ Fahad

c. *Nariman House*
   i) Imran Babbar @ Imran @ Kasha
   ii) Umar

Names of Pak-based handlers figuring in the conversations (phonetic)

a. *Nariman House*
   i) Wassi
   ii) Zarar
   iii) Jundal
   iv) Buzurg
   v) Major General

b. *Hotel Oberoi*
   i) Kafa
   ii) Wassi
   iii) Zarar

c. *Hotel Taj*

i) Wassi

From Annexure-VII of Indo-Pak Dossier

[Some selected intercepted Conversation (locations and name etc. have been indicated on the basis of internal evidence of conversations)]

Hotel Taj Mahal 27.11.2008: 0310 hrs

Receiver: Greetings!

Caller: Greetings! There are three Ministers and one Secretary of the Cabinet in your hotel. We don't know which room.

Receiver: Oh! That is good news. It is the icing on the cake.

Caller: Find those 3-4 persons and get whatever you want from India

Nariman House: 27.11.2008: 1945 hrs

Caller: Greetings. What did the Major General say?

Receiver: Greetings. The Major General directed us to do what we like. We should not worry. The operation has to be concluded tomorrow morning. Pray to God. Keep two magazines and three grenades aside, and expend the rest of your ammunition.

Hotel Taj Mahal: 27.11.2008: 0126 hrs

Caller: Are you setting the fire or not?

Receiver: Not yet. I am getting a mattress ready for buring.

The days following 26/11

AS EXPECTED, THE next two to three days were really hectic, with me running from one meeting to another with different sets of senior management from the Security establishment. Notices for different types of discussions in both Houses of Parliament were pouring in, in sheaves so that it was difficult to keep count of them. We started preparing to enable the Home Minister to calibrate his responses in both Houses of Parliament as per the laid-down procedure.

However, one thing which repeatedly came up, which could not be ignored was that we had the intelligence inputs on a possible attack from the coastal route. Several coastal security establishments had sensed the threat and were in preparation for meeting the challenges. But it became clear during the series of meetings happening in the MHA that there had been apparently some intervention from the top most political office, instructing 'restraint' in the counter-initiatives to avert such attacks.

This was on account of the oft-repeated statements of the

intelligence and security establishment managers.

We soon realised that while the top brass intervening in the regular security procedures would never be exposed before the public, the intelligence and security establishments would be blamed for abject failure although they had done their professional work in an exemplary and outstanding manner. We all knew it. We all knew that these establishments have actually prevented many an evil design; many a potential terror attack has been averted by their sheer diligence and professionalism, a matter not in the public domain.

We had seen it before. We also saw the same thing happening again, when a similar attack by an ISI-sponsored group was foiled by the Indian Coast Guard few years later when the ruling dispensation had changed. Little wonder, the entire security establishment has been angry for the past ten years. They have been branded 'a failure' for political reasons. It is not that I am stating this for the first time, I said this long before many others suspected and said this.

A press clipping https://www.dawn.com/news/443698/mumbai-attackers-got-internal-help-modi will support this:

> **Mumbai attackers got internal help: Modi**
> Jawed Naqvi
> February 09, 2009, *The Dawn,* a Pakistani Daily Newspaper:
> NEW DELHI, Feb 8: Indian politics was stranded between a hawk and a turncoat on Sunday, when its chief ideologue for military solutions against terrorism, which mostly also includes Islamabad, suddenly blamed 'internal help' for Mumbai's November nightmare. The ruling Congress party, missing the message, found itself unable to row back from its politically risky standoff with Pakistan.
> As senior Congress leaders continued to chart a hawkish course against Pakistan for the 26 November attacks, Gujarat Chief Minister Narendra Singh Modi, a mentor of national

jingoism, hinted at an internal hand in the terror strikes. 'If we single out that one incident (of the Mumbai attacks) and ask any person in this country, even with basic information and knowledge, they will say that such a big terror attack on India cannot take place without any internal help from the nation itself', Mr Modi told a national meeting of the main opposition Bharatiya Janata Party (BJP) in Nagpur.

'I want to know who is stopping them from taking action.... This is because of vote bank politics', Mr Modi told BJP's National Council meeting alleging that all policies of the ruling coalition are driven by the appeasement of Indian Muslims.

The communal barb notwithstanding, Mr Modi's claim is expected to considerably ease the pressure on Pakistan. Some analysts felt his comments were similar to the leaked findings into the Mumbai incident which Pakistan has concluded and may make public any time.

Mr Modi's comments came three weeks after he attacked the Congress party-led coalition government for asking Pakistan to accept the statement of Ajmal Amir Kasab, lone terrorist caught alive for Mumbai attacks, as proof of what happened and how India itself 'does not have a similar provision under its laws' to accept a confession made to police.

Talking of zero tolerance to terrorism, he regretted that the last few years had witnessed a series of such incidents.

Analysts said Mr Modi's new theory on the November attacks contradicts India's official position. India has maintained that the conspiracy was entirely plotted in Pakistan. In fact, India has supplied a dossier of 'proof' to Pakistan making the same point.

'Mr Modi's remarks, though an attempt to politicise the attacks along communal lines, is poorly timed as they have been made just 24 hours ahead of Pakistan's reply to the 26/11 dossier of proof', said one Indian report.

'The Pakistani establishment will look at Modi's statement very carefully as it provides them the necessary room to evade taking direct responsibility for the 26/11 attacks.'

In New Delhi, Congress president Sonia Gandhi issued a veiled warning to Pakistan, saying those abetting terrorism in India from across the borders will be given a 'befitting reply' and they should not construe New Delhi's 'restraint' as weakness.

Describing terrorism as one of the major challenges, Ms Gandhi said:

'The recent barbaric terror attacks of Mumbai and Assam remind us of the pain we are going through. But we have no doubt that we will overcome this difficult situation.'

Indian Foreign Minister Pranab Mukherjee, who is due to hold discussions in Dhaka on Monday with the new Bangladeshi government, was expected to raise the issue of terrorism allegedly emanating from there. India has not publicly accepted Pakistani reports that a Bangladesh-based group could be involved in the Mumbai attacks.

Speaking at a conclave of Congress district and block level office-bearers in New Delhi, and evidently unmindful of Mr Modi's latest views on Mumbai, Mr Mukherjee warned that India had kept all options open to deal with terrorism he believes emanates from Pakistan.

'Perpetrators of (Mumbai) terror attacks must be punished. Nobody should think that this country is helpless and cannot tackle the situation arising out of terrorism', Mr Mukherjee said.

'I repeat all options are open', he said and asserted that terrorism would be fought with 'courage and fortitude'.

'This menace has to be confronted and we are exactly doing that.'

He said India had asked Pakistan to fulfil its own commitments that terrorists would not use its land.

'Don't try to divert the attention of the international community. Take corrective measures and don't think that you can simply shirk this responsibility', he told Pakistan.

In fact, I was a henchman for the Ministry of Home Affairs, Internal Security Division at that time. It is in my knowledge that many terror attacks had been averted due to the professionalism of the Indian security agencies. I had, in fact, said so in the Allahabad High Court on 4/5 January 2008 in response to a suo motu cognisance by the Court seeking response of the Union of India, MHA on the attacks on District Court premises in three places in UP that occurred in November 2007. I would like to quote from this affidavit:

> There exists an effective coordination mechanism for sharing of information about terrorist attacks and other challenges to internal security. Any available information about plans of terrorist groups to carry out attacks is shared by the Central security and intelligence agencies with the State Police authorities from time to time. The State Police on account of their spread on the ground is to develop on such information and take appropriate counter measures including preventive action, against such possible terrorist strikes. There is a continuous process and channel of communication between the Central and State agencies, and advisories on the possible threats, reinforcement of security arrangements etc. are issued by the central security agencies from time to time.

I have filed it on affirmation. I know the capacity of our security agencies. Only if they are allowed to function freely, they can work wonders. But autonomy is what they lack. We should trust them.

The intervention from some top office in the country had rendered the security forces ineffective in spite of their proven capabilities. An excellent bunch of resource had to take the flak, look like an incompetent bunch of failed personnel. Their seething anger was legitimate. They knew they could have prevented the Mumbai attacks. Their hands were tied.

In fact, such frenzy was seen in the MHA that on 30.11.2008, when I was at a wedding at the Uttara Guruvayoorappan temple in Mayur Vihar, I received a call from the office to report immediately. As soon as I reached the MHA conference room in North Block, I found a huge posse of senior officers gathered there and we were informed that the Home Minister had resigned and we would have a new Union Home Minister.

But certain questions that keep agitating me and I am still seeking answers to are:

How did the 10 terrorist who got dropped few kms off the Colaba coastline manage to find their way and come to Badhwar Park?

How did the terrorists find their way to Leopold cafe, CST, Taj Mahal Hotel, or Trident or wherever, without any local guide?

We all know how difficult it is to find our way through our metros, traffic, encroachments and reach our destinations without local support, it is a miracle despite all the electronic support at one's command.

There had been repeated sharing of intelligence with the Chief Secretary, Maharashtra and his next in command, Additional Chief Secretary (Home), who was at the Taj Hotel. What was she doing that day at Taj Mahal Hotel when she had access to overwhelming actionable intelligence on the possibility of attacks at such places?

In context of this case, I would like to share a confession by an intelligence officer after such incidents as Ishrat Jahan, Sohrabuddin Sheikh etc. took place—those in the know of intelligence simply pass on the information to operational units and also ensure that they and their families do not go near the targeted spots, lest they suffer undesirable consequences like Rajinder Kumar and others. *But Zutshi was there in spite of being privy to overwhelming inputs. Was she there at some political master's behest?*

Moreover, she escaped unscathed. The communication records show that more important the target—like any cabinet minister of high rank—s/he was destined to be the terrorists' leverage point. How did Zutshi come out unscathed? *Who was with her, who too must have escaped? Could they be ministers/a minster (the transcripts say there were three wazirs/ministers in the premises)?*

On balance of considerations of the above, my friend Peter was not off the mark when he said, *inaugurate karne gayee thi kya, madam?*

Ajmal Kasab had been caught alive. The investigations subsequently were leading to a Pakistani involvement. *At this juncture, the then Minister of Minorities Affairs in the Union Cabinet and a senior politician, A R Antulay gives an interview to* India Today, *which talks of the conspiracy to kill his favourite police officer, trying to digress, and undermine the whole investigative process. What was the agenda he was pursuing?*

PC as Home Minister

ON 1 DECEMBER 2008, P Chidambaram took office as the new Home Minister. He had the tenacity to hype whatever steps he would take. He did join with a bang. He was rated as efficient, progressive, result-oriented, media savvy and eminent as a lawyer and all the precious adjectives in the dictionary were applied to describe him by the media and others while welcoming him.

Some of the immediate initiatives announced by the new Home Minister were: The government notified the Unlawful Activities (Prevention) Amendment Act, 2008 and the National Investigation Agency Act, 2008 on 31.12.2008 to reinforce the legal and punitive provisions of law to combat terrorism by amending the Unlawful Activities (Prevention) Act, 1967.

The last amendment to the UAP Act had been in September 2004 through an ordinance, later ratified in November 2004 as replacement to the POTA (Prevention of Terrorism Act) of the previous regime (the A B Vajpayee government).

Chidambaram publicised introduction of more stringent

sections of the Act as legislative measures to counter terror. Till the period preceding the 2008 Mumbai attacks, the UPA's position on any amendment to the UAPA was 'not acceptable', in spite of several international agencies like the CTED suggesting such amendments.

The Counter-Terrorism Executive Directorate (CTED) of the UN Security Council had visited India in November 2006. The officers of the CTED, after meeting with officers of various ministries and organisations including the MHA, had prepared a report, inter alia, covering various aspects of India's institutional, legal, practical application and capabilities regarding counter-terrorism. Some of the suggestions made by the CTED were:

Comprehensive counter-terrorism law

> Recruitment by terrorist groups should be specifically criminalised under UAPA.
> Section 40 of the UAPA should apply to unlisted terrorist organisations as well. At present, section 40 applies to 'terrorist organisations' and section 2 (m) of UAPA defines 'terrorist organisation' as an organisation listed in the schedule or an organisation operating under the same name as an organisation so listed.
> It is also recommended that section 40 should also apply for individual terrorist.
> Section 17 of UAPA should also criminalise provision of funds.

UAPA as enacted in 2004 provided for action against individuals raising fund for a terrorist organisation. 'Terrorist organisation' was defined under section 2(m). The CTED said that this section should also be extended to raising of fund for any terrorist organisation, whether declared under section 2(m) or not—meaning in case an organisation has been found to be involved in terrorist activities and not yet been defined as per provision of section 2(m)—which involves detailed procedure including assessment by a tribunal headed by a serving judge of a High Court, with public consultation etc. This is a time-consuming process.

Further CTED also recommended that raising of funds to be given to a individual terrorist, also should be included under the ambit of this section.

The CTED, in its report, had also recommended that, 'India should ensure that counter-terrorism cases are handled within a reasonable time frame, by judges who specialise in this field'. It is felt that this can, perhaps, be taken care of by bringing in a provision under UAPA, to try such cases only by a special courts/ fast track courts, the CTED said. It suggested, India should:

> Criminalise the willful provision or collection, by any means, directly or indirectly, of funds by their nationals or in their territories with the intention that the funds should be used, or in the knowledge that they are to be used, in order to carry out terrorist acts (para 1 (b) of UN Security Council Resolution 1373).
> The incorporation of para 1 (c) and 1 (d) of U.N. Security Council Resolution 1373 may also be considered.
> Copy of UN Security Council Resolution 1373 is enclosed.

Funds are described as 'assets of every kind, whether tangible or intangible, movable or immovable, however, acquired, and legal documents or instruments in any form, including electronic or digital, evidencing title to, or interest in, such assets, including, but not limited to, bank credits, travellers cheques, bank cheques, money orders, shares, securities, bonds, drafts, letters of credit'.

The same definition may be used for defining 'property'. The above definition of 'fund' is based on the definition of 'fund' as provided by the International Convention for Suppression of Financing of Terrorism, the use of this definition is enshrined in the Essential Criteria of Special Recommendation-II of the Financial Action Task Force.

Chidambaram's second initiative was the National Investigation Agency Act.

Let us get it right. The National Investigation Agency was not a new idea. The Supreme Court had on 21.9.2006 directed setting up of a Federal Agency to investigate offences having ramifications across various States, as well as across boundaries of the country in the *Prakash Singh versus Union of India* case. There had been several committees like the Malimath Committee, the Madhav Menon Committee etc. which had recommended setting up of such an agency. The Eighth Report of the Second Administrative Reforms Commission had inter alia recommended setting up of such an agency.

However, prior to the new Home Minister taking over, the then uninterested Home Minister, Shivraj Patil, was never favourably disposed to the idea. He held a series of meetings with several dignitaries after receipt of the Eighth Report of the Second Administrative Reforms Commission as well as pursuant to the Supreme Court Order, finding ways and means not to accept the recommendations on such an agency.

A government Affidavit before the Supreme Court in *Prakash Singh Versus Union of India* case is:

> It is submitted that the Union of India continued to make various efforts to expedite the process of consultation with the State Governments. However, as only few States had responded and the period of 12 weeks was to expire on 10th July 2007, an application for further extension of time of 12 weeks was filed to finalise views of the Union Government. It is submitted that despite persistent follow up, a number of States were still to give their views and hence an application for further extension of time of 12 weeks was filed on 4th October 2007 to finalise the views of the Union Government. In deference to the order of this Hon'ble Court, the Union

Government has been steadfastly pursuing the matter with the State Governments, so as to obtain their views at the earliest. Towards this end, the Ministry of Home Affairs has sought the views of all States and Union Territories and has also, inter alia, endorsed copies of views furnished by the NHRC, Soli Sorabjee Committee and the BPR&D, to all the States and Union Territories.

It is further submitted that the subject of 'Central Law Enforcement Agency/Federal Investigation Agency' was taken up for detailed and intensive discussion in the meeting of the Parliamentary Consultative Committee for the Ministry of Home Affairs, in its meeting held on November 29, 2007. It is also submitted that this subject matter was also discussed in the meeting with the Chief Ministers on Internal Security held on December 20, 2007. Following this, further communications have also been addressed to all the State Governments by the Union Home Secretary.

It is respectfully submitted that the subject involves important legal and constitutional issues and implementational intricacies. Therefore, apart from the need for examination and consideration of these aspects in consultation with the concerned Ministries/agencies, it is, inter alia, also necessary to develop a consensus with the State Governments. All efforts in this direction are being made, but it has not been possible to arrive at a conclusive view in the matter. Therefore, further time would be required by the Union of India to be able to submit its views on the issue outlined in paragraphs 32 and 33 of the order dated September 22, 2006 passed by the Hon'ble Court.

Safe passage of two Security Bills

The new Home Minister took it upon himself to get the two relevant Bills passed in Parliament and these were the proposed amendments to the Unlawful Activities (Prevention) Amendment Bill and the National Investigation Agency Bill. Working continuously for three days, MHA officials and Law Ministry officials brought a proposal before the Cabinet by 5 December 2008 and it was cleared by the Cabinet within days.

No more requests from the Minister of Defence's office seeking more time. The then Defence Minister, A K Antony, had the habit of seeking more time for framing his ministries' views—like when CCS approval was sought to the approach to Indian position in the Home Secretary Level Talks in 2008.

In so far as legislative exercises are concerned, after approval by the Cabinet, there is an elaborate exercise by the government itself. The piloting ministry/ies—which was MHA in this case and Law Ministry (involving its Department of Legal Affairs and Legislative Department), involved in iterating the contents of the Bills—ensure to the last detail that the policy of the government is in real terms translated into the Bills. During this period, my seniors and I had lost touch with the essential bodily requirement called sleep.

The Bills were introduced in Parliament in the second week of December in 2008. The introduction of the Bills was very close to the seventh anniversary of the attack on Parliament and on the 13th, the Bills were sent to the President of India, Pratibha Patil, seeking her permission to lay these two Bills before the Houses, as mandated by Constitution Article 117 (3) for the NIA Bill. I remember these dates particularly clearly because on 13 December 2001, I was working on deputation with the Lok Sabha Secretariat and was inside the Parliament House at that time. This is only a small detail. But through the process of drafting of the Bills as well as its consideration by the Cabinet, its introduction in the Lok Sabha, I felt a sense of poetic justice being rendered to me personally. I did not realise that this sense of inner elation was not to last for long.

In order to get the Bills ready to be presented to Parliament, an enormous effort as well as elaborate procedural requirements coupled with drafting of replies to questions in both the Houses, answering notices which were received with the Internal Security Division, preparing reports on the progress in respect to investigation and other activities related to 26/11 which triggered this, was needed. We had little time for our families; I did not even look at my son's face, he had come home for his winter vacations, which had been advanced due to some cyclonic disturbances in Chennai in the last week of November 2008.

We had little time to follow up on the responses/reports from several agencies during this period. Five or six Public Interest Litigations were filed in the Bombay High Court to which the government had to file its affidavits by 17th or 18th December 2008. Appreciating the volume of work, the Home Secretary instructed my senior, the Director (IS), to attend to these litigations (although the gentleman was no less busy) and also requested Gopal Subramaniam, the Additional Solicitor General, to appear in these cases. The Director (IS) and Gopal Subramaniam appeared before the Bombay High Court on the appointed date.

Concurrently, the Home Minister also initiated several purportedly 'strengthening measures' which included the strengthening of the coast through the Coastal Security Scheme in which the Central government offered assistance to set up coastal police stations in the coastal States, Desert policing to meet the unique demands of the desert terrain, Mega City policing, raising of new battalions in Central Paramilitary Forces, Amendment to the CISF Act to enable private establishments to engage CISF deployment on commercial terms, intelligence strengthening mechanisms, NATGRID, NCTC etc. This included revitalising some of the existing measures and recalibrating some ongoing measures and introducing some new steps.

Extract of affidavit filed on behalf of the Union of India in Bombay High Court in a PIL in February 2009:

> *National Security Guard:*
>
> The National Security Guard (hereinafter referred to as 'NSG') is a very effective counter terrorist force of our country. Therefore, various steps have been initiated to remove logistical weaknesses in mobilising and deploying NSG. Moreover, a decision has been taken to locate NSG units in a few regional hubs (like Bangalore, Chennai, Kolkata, Mumbai etc.) in the first instance, and also to draw upon the Commando Units of the Armed Forces to create more regional hubs. Further, in order to strengthen the capabilities of the States, Indian Reserve Battalions are being raised in most of the States with financial assistance from the answering Respondent. The Central Government has authorised that two Coys. of each such battalion may be raised as Special Commando Units for which additional assistance will be provided for training equipment, etc. In addition it has also been decided to set up 20 Counter Insurgency and Anti-Terrorism Schools in different parts of the country for training Commando Units of the State Police. Thus, the answering Respondent submits that these measures are in fact a step towards strengthening of the response mechanism as a part of a comprehensive crisis management plan to deal with the acts of terror and other security breaches, disaster etc. Further, the Ministry of Civil Aviation has issued a Notification dated 22 January 2009 under the provisions of the Aircraft Act, 1934 empowering an authorised officer to requisition an aircraft in the interest of public safety from an operator registered in India. Such an officer shall not be below the rank of Joint Secretary to the Government of India. Besides this, the Director General of National Security Guards has also been authorised vide Notification dated 23.1.2009 to do the same. This step has been taken to enable National Security Guards to get an aircraft at a short notice for moving its commandos for anti-terrorist operations anywhere in the country.

Coastal Security:

India has a coastline of 7,516.6 kilometers running through 13 States, namely, Gujarat, Maharashtra, Goa, Karnataka, Kerala, Tamil Nadu, Andhra Pradesh, Orissa and West Bengal and the Union Territories of Daman and Diu, Pondicherry, Lakshadweep and Andaman and Nicobar Islands (hereinafter referred to as 'Coastal States/Union Territories').

In order to ensure coastal security, steps are being undertaken for effective implementation of the 'Coastal Security Scheme'. The Coastal Security Scheme of the Ministry of Home Affairs is a scheme to assist 9 coastal States and 4 Union Territories in strengthening their infrastructure for coastal patrolling and surveillance.

This Scheme was formulated and approved by the answering Respondent in the year 2005 and has been under implementation, with a budgetary allocation of Rs 400 crore for non-recurring expenditure and Rs 151 crore over a period of five years for recurring expenditure (such as fuel, repair and maintenance of boats and training of manpower) for the entire period of five years.

It is stated and submitted that a decision has been taken to review the above scheme and to integrate it into a larger security system.

Further, it has also been decided that a Coastal Command would be created for overall supervision and coordination of maritime and coastal security with a mandate to secure the country's coastline.

It is stated and submitted that the answering Respondent is considering standardisation of issuance of identity cards to all fishermen and sea-faring personnel by implementing an effective system of mandatory registration of all types of fishing boats by the coastal States/Union Territories and also by optimal use of technology (operational details are not being disclosed) on these boats for effective monitoring and regulation of their movements.

Port Security:

In relation to this aspect, the answering Respondent states and submits that decisions have been taken. Interceptor boats at each Port, and a Marine Commando Unit would be placed there. Besides these measures, it has also been decided that Bomb Detection and Special Squads would also be placed at these Ports and identity cards would be issued to the staff and workers at the Ports. Further, it is stated and submitted that the possibility of carrying out customs and immigration facilities at the anchorage are being explored.

Operation SWAN (Joint Coastal Patrolling of Gujarat and Maharashtra Coast):

(i) In the year 1993, a three-tier surveillance mechanism for Gujarat and Maharashtra was introduced. The surveillance mechanism involved intensive surveillance of high seas, surveillance in territorial waters and patrolling in shallow waters along the shore. The surveillance on high seas is carried out by Navy and Coast Guard and patrolling of territorial waters is done by Coast Guard with Coast Guard vessels and aerial surveillance by Coast Guard aircrafts. A close coastal patrolling is done by deploying trawlers hired by Governments of Gujarat and Maharashtra and manned by personnel from Navy, Customs and Police.

(ii) In the year 2005-2006, a scheme was formulated to provide assistance to Coast Guard by the Ministry of Home Affairs postulating procurement of 15 interceptor boats and setting up of three Coast Guard Stations (2 in Maharashtra and 1 in Gujarat) with an estimated budged of Rs 342.6 crore, in order to make available speed boats for surveillance instead of trawlers as referred above. In fact, the process of construction of interceptor boats has been undertaken on a priority basis and land for Coast Guard Stations at Dhanu, Muru, Janjira and Beraval has been finalised.

City Surveillance:

(i) The answering Respondent states and submits that it is necessary that stricter norms are put in place for allowing foreigners to enter the State. For the said purpose, various entry points namely, the airports, the docks, the toll borders etc. should tighten their screening process. However, it is pertinent to note that the legal framework governing this issue is contained in the Passport (Entry to India) Act, 1920, Foreigners Act, 1946 and Registration of Foreigners Act, 1949. In terms of the Passport (Entry to India) Act, 1920, the foreigners coming to India are required to get visas from Indian Missions. The power to prohibit, regulate or restrict the entry of foreigners into India or their departure therefrom or their presence or continued presence therein is vested with the Central Government under Section 3 of Foreigners Act, 1946. Section 3(2)(c) of the Foreigners Act, 1946 empowers the Central Government to issue orders providing that the foreigner 'shall not remain in India or in any other prescribed area therein'. Further, in terms of Section 3(2)(e) of the Foreigners Act, 1946 read with para 11(2) of the Foreigners Order, 1948, Central Government has the powers to issue orders requiring the foreigner to reside in a particular place and imposing restrictions on his movements. These powers of the Central Government have been delegated to all the State Governments & UT Administrations vide Notification SO No.590 dated 19 April 1958. The State Governments/UT Administrations have full powers to deport any foreign national under the delegated powers. The detection and deportation of illegally staying foreign nationals in India is an ongoing process. The Registration of Foreigners Act, 1939 and the Registration of Foreigners Rules, 1992 mandate that certain category of foreigners whose intended stay in India is more than 180 days, or those who require registration as per their visa authorization, are to get themselves registered with the Registration Officer within a period of 14 days from the date of arrival. However, Afghan nationals are required to get themselves registered within 7 days and Pakistan nationals within 24 hours of their arrival.

(ii) In addition, the institutional framework for discharging the sovereign function of immigration comprises of 76 immigration check posts (ICPs) in the country of which 24 are airport ICPs, 20 sea port ICPs and 32 land ICPs. Modernisation of 33 land ICPs which regulates 98.5% of the passenger traffic in phase I has already been initiated and substantial progress has been made in installation of hardware and software to facilitate the above modernization which includes – upgradation of computer systems, installation of passport reading machines, upgradation of Central Foreign Bureau, and foreign regional registration offices to facilitate data sharing for expeditious and prompt action by the immigration authorities, implementation of Advanced Passengers Automation System at 6 international airports, namely, Delhi, Mumbai, Chennai, Bangalore, Hyderabad and Cochin to effectively reduce immigration clearance time and enhance the security screening of passengers, 1800 additional posts have been sanctioned to strengthen the manpower to complement the Bureau of Immigration to achieve the aforesaid task. Besides this, networking of the ICPs has also been planned and the same would be implemented in the year 2009-2010. In order to further improve the effectiveness of the immigration system, the existing initiative of modernization/upgradation of infrastructure and equipments has been integrated into Mission Mode Project (MMP) and a Detailed Project Report (DPR) for the MMP – 'Immigration, Visa and 'Foreigners Registration and Tracking' (FRT) is under preparation. The MMP would provide an integrated framework for visa, immigration, and FRT processes under this project with focus on core values of security, facilitation and enablement. This MMP would also comprehensively address issues related to illegal immigration through legitimate entry routes like person travelling with invalid documents, overstay of foreigners, misuse of visa, etc. In order to strengthen and augment the intelligence machinery action has already been taken by way of sanctioning additional posts, and steps are being taken to fill the vacancies in an expeditious manner. This will also enable strengthening of the institutional mechanisms for gathering, analysis and sharing of intelligence and operational coordination among the agencies and the States.

(iii) Further action has been taken to strengthen the Special Branches/ Intelligence Agencies in the States/UTs by providing assistance under the Scheme for Modernisation of State Police Forces (also refer Para 7) and 5% of funding under the Scheme has been earmarked for this purpose. In recognition of the urgent need for strengthening the State Special Branches it has been decided to have a separate Sub-Scheme for this purpose, the detailed parameters of which are being finalized.

(iv) Steps have also been initiated to strengthen the State Special Branches, a draft scheme in respect of which has already been circulated to States. In addition, connectivity between the Multi-Agency Centre and the State Special Branches through State Intelligence Bureau is being strengthened by way of dedicated and secure connections and data centres.

Presidential Assent

The Bills were passed in both Houses of Parliament and the exercise with the Parliament concluded by 20 December 2008.

Subsequent to passage of the Bills by Parliament, an elaborate exercise was conducted jointly by the piloting ministry (MHA) and the Law Ministry. After the passage of Bills and authentication from the Lok Sabha Secretariat, the Bills were received in the Law Ministry on 23rd or 24th of December 2008.

For any Bill, these steps are a must. At the first stage, the Law Ministry's Legislative Department makes a tentative draft, and sends the Bill to the piloting Ministry. The Piloting Ministry (MHA in this case) examines the Bill as passed by Parliament and confirms that the public interest objectives and commensurate policy set out at the time of initiating the proposal have been covered in the Bill. After appropriate approvals including that of the Union Minister (Home Minister in this case), this exercise was conducted and completed by the Home Ministry on 26 and 27 December 2008. After all approvals, including the Union Home Minister's approval, the Bill was sent to the Law Minister for obtaining the Presidential Assent. The objectives are appropriately captured in the text of the Bills as passed by Parliament.

On 30.12.2008 in the evening, the Law Ministry told the Joint Secretary (IS) that the Bills were fit for Presidential Assent, and the ministry wanted a last-minute reiteration meeting. The Joint Secretary (IS) and I reached the Law Ministry at about 8:00 pm. The meeting went on up to 9:30 pm. After this, the Law Ministry suggested that I drop the file for Presidential Assent at the Rashtrapati Bhavan. I was to be accompanied by a staffer from the Law Ministry, who was conversant with the work process in the Rashtrapati Bhavan.

I had driven in my own car to the Law Ministry that evening as I had planned to go home directly from Shastri Bhavan. The ministry official, a person called Sharma, also stayed in my neighbourhood and he requested me to drop him at Dwarka Mor after our Rashtrapati Bhavan visit. I readily agreed.

Slapped by a ghost

We reached the Rashtrapati Bhavan at about 10 pm. I was

received by Subramaniam, a Section Officer in the Rashtrapati Bhavan. As we shared the name, he was very cordial. After completing the formalities, the Law Ministry staffer and I drove down to Dwarka Mor where I dropped him.

The Joint Secretary (IS) was anxious to ensure no hiccups and called me up at 10:52 pm when I was driving, to confirm that the papers had been dropped at Rashtrapati Bhavan. The anxiety was on account of the fact that the President was in Visakhapatnam or some such place and one of the officers of the President's Secretariat was to fly down next morning to get her assent for the Bills.

I dropped the Law Ministry staffer at Dwarka Mor T Point and took a U turn to return home. At this point in time, I noticed I was being followed by four bikes. I thought, this was a pre-New Year prank. Some kids might be high and just indulging in childish pranks. But, soon, it was clear to me that something more sinister was going on behind me. These four bikes, each had two riders (one rider and one pillion each). And they were persistent in keeping behind, dodging me.

When I reached the Sector 16-B police post (which has since been shifted), I made up my mind to seek their help. It was a new car I was driving. I had bought it on Christmas day. The papers were not ready. I also did not have a Parking Sticker, which itself is a power statement in Delhi. I had thought that in a few days, New Year will dawn and I will get a 2009 sticker.

When I tried to enter the police post, which was a single room post at the entrance, I was stopped by a Delhi police staffer and abused. He said, 'everyone here is a Home Ministry officer'. The fellows who were chasing me had gone behind the police post, presumably to pretend to urinate. This police staffer asked for my license. When I was trying to retrieve my wallet, the policeman took away Rs 1,000 and some more notes which were in the wallet. Meanwhile, he continued to abuse me.

Typically, Delhi, my readers must be thinking. The situation was getting bad to worse.

In a flash I decided what to do. I seized an opportunity and got into my car and started driving like mad. Since I knew that the men chasing me would not give up and would continue to pursue me, instead of turning left on Road No.201, I went straight towards Sector 12, took a turn left into Sector 4, took another turn at Modern Convent School. From then onward, I took a right turn and reached Lovely Chowk near my apartment. I reached home at about 11:55 pm.

My mother was in our house on that day. She had the habit of waking up, no matter what time I returned. After washing up, when I sat down to eat the dinner my wife had warmed up, my mother came out of her room and, as was the normal practice, came up to serve me some small morsel of some delicacy on the menu, just to satisfy herself, that she had fed her son. In fact, my wife often told her that she would not let Amma's baby (I am the youngest child) remain hungry. But that day, my mother looked at my face and commented in Tamil, *'Ennadda pei aranjaa madiri irrukka'* (you look like having been slapped by a ghost). A mother surely has a sixth sense about danger to her offspring, whatever be her age.

First thing in the morning, I went and dropped my mother at my sister-in-law's home to avoid her smelling something untoward. Then I went to office and reported the episode to the department. The sequence of events were reduced to writing. The report was then brought to the notice of the Home Secretary who remarked that this was 'unacceptable' and opined that we should write to the Commissioner of Police.

Following the receipt of Presidential assent for the two new Bills, they had to be printed in the form of a Gazette Notification at the Government of India Press. A colleague and close friend, who was a national football referee, in the true spirit of team work agreed to get the notification printed in the Gazette for me by following up with the Government Press at Mayapuri, New Delhi to ensure publication of this Gazette Notification on that very day.

I, meanwhile, had to devote myself to drafting a communication and modifying it quite a few times, so that a report in the form of a letter from the Special Secretary (Internal Security), could be sent to the then Commissioner of Police. This letter from the Special Secretary (Internal Security), to the then Commissioner of Police was sent on 19 January 2009, detailing the incident as well as calling for a detailed investigation. That is after Kasab's identity as Pakistani national had been accepted by Pakistan. A serving MHA officer was being intimidated. What if I had been carrying important official papers? I had been transporting such documents, just an hour before being chased by unknown men.

Ministers, some mandarins and the MHA

THE NATIONAL INVESTIGATION Agency Act and Unlawful Activities (prevention) Amendment Act were notified on 1.1.2009, meeting the timeline set by Minister Chidambaram. We were all so engrossed in the work on the new initiatives, little did we realise that we had not been following up on the status of investigation of 26/11 or for that matter, any other case.

Meanwhile, reports received from various agencies, including the Mumbai Police and ATS (whatever was left of it), were put together and perused. The first time any written document was received in the Ministry of Home Affairs stating that Ajmal Kasab, the lone surviving terrorist of Mumbai attack of 26/11, was a Pakistani was on 7 January 2009. Prior to this, the information had all been in the newspapers and television. The reason why I am recalling this information is because this is connected to the attack on me personally just before the New Year.

The new Home Minister had also convened a Chief

Minister's Conference on Internal Security on 6.1.2009 to disseminate to the States the initiatives being taken by the Government of India in the aftermath of 26/11. Generally, a Chief Minister's Conference on Internal Security is handled by the Internal Security Division of the MHA. But this time, this conference was assigned to the Central State Division. I was sent to Karnataka on some official duty and do not have any insights into the deliberations in the meeting, except that the Prime Minister attended the CMs' meet.

Chidambaram's infrastructural initiatives were assigned to different programme Divisions in the MHA—like Coastal policing to Border Management (Coastal Security) Division, Desert and Mega City policing to be handled by the Police Modernisation Division etc.

A great deal of hype was created both within the government and outside, as if the government had launched a direct attack against terrorism. Those reading the finer print, however, knew there was more noise than action. Central intentions did not match State government abilities, Central allocations did not sync with State efforts. Take one small initiative. Boats were provided for patrolling the coast to State governments without them providing the personnel to man these vessels; no specialised training on monitoring the seas was ever envisaged. It was the same with other hyped schemes like the Mega City policing or Desert policing plans.

The much-touted CCTNS (Crime and Criminal Tracking Network System) suffered an inherent implementation design defect, a faulty milestones scheduling. Every agency breached the target date. Yet, I am sure, today it must be a much better system than the ICPA (Integrated Common Police Application), an archaic one which it replaced.

In 2009, even the engagement of Public Prosecutor became a matter of endless discussion and dissent. Many of the

IS Division officers had suggested the name of the renowned Mumbai-based criminal lawyer Deepak Salvi, who had been the Public Prosecutor in the 1993 Mumbai blast case. In September 2017, his contribution to justice[10] in the 1993 case trial was well acknowledged and placed on record by the judicial officer. Personally, we all knew him as an individual of impeccable integrity. But the NIA team would not have him. NIA officials brought in another name, Rohini Salian. Salian had been with the Central Bureau of Investigation and closely associated with the team of officers who had joined the NIA.

It later transpired that Salian was brough in to help NIA further the narrative of the then government. However, in 2015, Salian went against the CBI position[11] when the NIA sought closure in the Malegaon case.

---

10 On 7 September 2017, a designated TADA court in Mumbai pronounced the quantum of sentence against five gangsters – Abu Salem, Mustafa Dossa, Mohammed Dossa, Firoz Abdul Rashid Khan and Karimullah Sheikh.
A death sentence was handed out to two and life sentences to the other three convicts in the attack that killed 257 persons and injured more than 700 in a serial bomb blast in the city in 1993.
'All the seven accused tried to thwart my attempts to bring them to book. They kept filing new applications every day. It was very challenging', Special Counsel D N Salvi told News18.

11 In the summer of 2015, the NIA denied her statement to *The Indian Express* that Salian had been asked to go 'soft' on the 2008 Malegaon blast case. Special public prosecutor Rohini Salian said she had given her statement a lot of thought.
Salian also disclosed that she wanted to seek discharge of nine Muslims, arrested and chargesheeted by the Maharashtra ATS and CBI for a 2006 blast in Malegaon. http://indianexpress.com/article/india/india-others/nia-asking-salian-to-go-soft-i-am-a-criminal-lawyer-not-stupid-to-say-this-without-proof/. All UAPA offences at the time of chargesheet Under Section 45, need government sanction. Which means that chargesheet has to be vetted and approved by Government of India which functionally makes NIA a caged parrot. If the new government has reviewed the sanction including the evidences brought out, such situations are bound to arise.

The National Investigation Agency

After the two Acts were notified, began the work of establishing an organisational structure for the National Investigation Agency. One of my many duties was to oversee the NIA formation. The first round of discussions on the structure of the NIA, naturally dealt with the procedure to be followed for appointment of a Director General for the NIA.

I had suggested that as per the laid-down procedure for such appointments, a search committee should be constituted. Once the search committee recommends the names of officers, the Home Minister could choose his man from the shortlist. Once the Minister made his preference known, we could obtain the required approvals for the appointing authority, which in this case, would be the Appointments Committee of the Cabinet (ACC).

There was disagreement on the procedure as laid down. The only issue was whether the DG appointment should be done by the Internal Security Division or the Police-I (IPS) Division which deals with appointments/ deployment and other cadre-controlling issues of the Indian Police Service. This question arose because the Act had provided that the DG of NIA shall be of the rank of Director General or Addl Director General of Police of a State government. Hence, the natural corollary was that a police officer would be appointed which was the domain of the Police-I Division.

In the third week of January, when the two respective Joint Secretaries were in the process of resolving the matter, came a surprise. We were told that a Director General for the National Investigating Agency had already been appointed.

The Internal Security Division had no clue to how and when this appointment was processed. Minister Chidambaram had hand-picked the man and had taken the ACC on board to appoint R V Raju (since deceased) as the DG, NIA. Raju was from the Jammu & Kashmir cadre of the IPS of the rank of Additional Director General of Police.

As the appointment was already made, though IS did not know about it, we started taking appropriate steps to issue the relevant orders relating to his conditions of service as per laid-down procedure. What was the procedure followed and how he was appointed was not known to the Internal Security Division. I can recall my counterpart from the Police Division asking me about the procedures followed for this appointment, once the media announced his name. We had to tell the Police Division, we did not know any details and this came as a surprise to the Police.

Needless to say, the two Joint Secretaries of both Divisions had been kept in the dark and did not like the way their domain had been breached by an overbearing Union Minister who had literally belittled their position, besides bringing to nought all the preparatory work the IS and Police Division had done on this count and spent considerable time and effort in this.

In order to understand the dynamics in these corridors of power, one has to appreciate and understand the intrinsic relationships that exist in such powerful ministries like the Ministry of Home Affairs.

This new Director General had been a direct choice of the Home Minister, who was overbearing, all-pervading, all-powerful with an illusory sense of having monopoly over wisdom. In the ministry he had established an aura of invincibility and integrity, so much so that , it is a matter of record that in a testament before a judge in the case of Ravi Dhiren Ghosh v/s NIA (relating to the trial of a man in a case of Fake Indian Currency in which I was called as a witness), I had issued the prosecution sanction and made a submission that the prosecution was approved by the then Home Minister, who is an eminent lawyer in his own right. In fact, the NIA got a conviction in the case, that can be corroborated from the order of the Special NIA Court which awarded verdict in this case in January 2014.[12]

The Minister's blue-eyed boy, Raju was just as overbearing as his patron. Even while his conditions of appointment were being drafted, this gentleman sought to entitle to himself items which were beyond the entitlements of an incumbent holding analogous position or in simple terms, his peers. Soon Raju was complaining to Chidambaram, I was the Division's 'biggest bogey man who shows him the Rule Book', every time he needed something. Anyway, the Minister, too, did not like me for various reasons and humiliated me often. Now I was in the bad books of the DG, NIA as well as his patron. The truth of the matter is, 'entitlements' in the ministries are codified/ standardised by the Department of Expenditure of the Ministry of Finance and any upward revision of budget necessarily requires clearance from them. These clearances do not come forth easily. Raju would get what his peer officers got and no more. I had nothing to do with this, except that I was the intermediary facilitating official, in his case. He decided to shoot the messenger. Fortunately, at that time, my seniors in the Internal Security Division and the Home Secretary himself protected me.

Soon, Raju started building his own team. The first three officers who were recruited in the NIA after the Director General had either a Kerala (home State of the DG) or J&K (cadre State of DG) connection. Lokanath Behara, the first Inspector General, was a Kerala cadre police officer. DIG S P Pani was a J&K cadre police officer. DIG Sajid Farid Shapoo was a Kashmiri police officer of MP cadre. I found their kowtowing to their boss unbearable but my seniors counselled silence.

---

12 https://timesofindia.indiatimes.com/india/Court-nails-Pak-govt-hand-in-fake-rupee-racket/articleshow/29787211.cms
http://www.rediff.com/news/report/terrorsim-in-a-first-life-term-for-6-accused-in-fake-currency-case/20140130.htm

I recall a meeting in the Union Public Service Commission regarding framing of Recruitment Rules (Recruitment Rules are standardised benchmarks that define one's eligibility for appointment to various posts) which Inspector General Behara and I attended. In spite of some of the legitimate concerns the UPSC officials raised, I managed to defend the NIA proposal successfully. The Inspector General was extremely thankful and said he would correct any misgivings with the DG and the Minister. I learnt that he had really gone and told the Minister that Internal Security Division had sent its best officer to get the Recruitment Rules passed by the UPSC.

However, I had had enough of the fledgling NIA and requested the Joint Secretary (Internal Security) to relieve me of the oversight of this institution. People were surprised. Normally, in any of the ministries in the government, nobody lets go of the power of functional oversight over an institution because this carries unstated perks and goodies. But the quest for power and chasing goodies was never my cup of tea.

Hindu Terror & NIA

If anyone recapitulates the investigation history of NIA through 2009-2010, it was all about introducing a new nonexistent 'Hindu Terrorism' concept. In every case assigned to NIA—from the Samjhauta Express Blasts, Malegaon to Ajmer Sharif—they overlooked the first set of evidences and replaced it with evidences supporting the Hindu Terror narrative.

The first major virgin case on which NIA claimed success is the case of some law and order disturbance between the participants in a rally on Diwali day in 2009, in which the Hindu Jagran Manch and Sanathan Sansthan were the participants. On 16.10.09, it was Diwali eve and a Narakasur effigy competition was held near the Shantadurga temple at Sancoale-Verna in Goa. The case report said, the accused persons and 'other persons known and unknown' conspired together to plant IEDs at the places of effigy competitions as they were against such competition and as part of their conspiracy, the above said group planted IEDs in a vehicle which was parked on the road near the Shantadurga temple on the night of 16.10.2009. Subsequently the vehicle was located and the bomb was diffused by the Verna police station.

NIA termed it 'a case of Hindu Terrorism'.

I have heard a lot of debates on national media channels and people speaking for and against the existence of any Hindu Terror. But many people do not know of the dots and those who know, fail to join the dots.

It was amply clear that under the garb of new initiatives, the new Home Minister had pulled wool over the nation's eyes. They were not his initiatives. For example a separate NIA-like mechanism had already been ordered by the apex court and the Administrative Reforms Commission in its VIIIth report titled 'Combating Terrorism' before Chidambaram's tenure as Home Minister began. The federal agency—which he said was long due and endeared himself to the Supreme Court—the NIA was actually used by the new Home Minister as an instrument to propagate a narrative of Hindu Terror, Saffron Terror etc. The lack of transparency in appointment of its first and second Directors General was very evident.

David Coleman Headley

At a distance of nearly a decade, the 'evidence' called 'David Coleman Headley' seems mythical. In popular memory, only the two differently coloured eyes remain. And we in India's security establishments know that there are not only two versions of the Headley story but several and Internal Security certainly does not know which is closest to the truth.

The NIA played a vital part in interrogation of the man

known to international media and security establishments as David Coleman Headley (born as Daood Sayed Gilani in Washington).

A man called Tahawwur Hussain Rana was a Pakistani Canadian resident of Chicago, USA who was an immigration service businessman and a former military physician. In 2011, he was convicted of providing support to the militant group Lashkar-e-Taiba and of allegedly plotting an attack on the Danish newspaper *Jyllands-Posten.* At the trial of Rana, an alleged co-conspirator, David Headley gave detailed information about the participation of Pakistan's Directorate of Inter-Services Intelligence (ISI) in carrying out the 26/11 Mumbai attacks.

Headley was arrested at Chicago's O'Hare International Airport while he was attempting to travel to Pakistan on 9 October 2009.

US authorities gave Indian investigators, ie, the then NIA, direct access to Headley. NIA was the investigating agency for terror cases in India. According to a report in the *Economic Times*, Meera Shankar, the then Indian ambassador to the US called on Union Home Minister P Chidambaram to discuss the agenda for his meeting (in September 2009) with United States Secretary of Homeland Security Janet Napolitano. She (Shankar) said: The Rana trial is going on and Headley is the key witness. The revelations coming out from the trial are shedding new light on the full details of the (26/11) conspiracy.

Since his guilty plea, Headley has cooperated with US and Indian authorities and given information about his associates. On 24 January 2013, a US federal court in Chicago sentenced Headley to 35 years in prison for his role in the Mumbai attacks.

The interrogation report of David Headley was submitted as a part of the 'tour' report of the investigating team, that is the NIA, then led by Inspector General Behara. The NIA submitted the 'tour' report to the Home Minister, P Chidambaram. The Home Minister's office is reported to have excised portions of the Headley testimony to NIA.

From custody in the USA, Headley later deposed in 'in camera' proceeding in the Abu Jundal case in India.[13]

During the online part of the trial in the Jundal case, Headley apparently said that Muzzamil Bhat (a key Kashmiri military asset of the LeT, according to the FBI) had told him that Muzzamil had played an important role in recruiting Ishrat Jahan and Pranesh Pillal alias Javed Mohammad Sheikh as fidayeen.[14] According to Headley, Muzzamil also claimed that he had been instrumental in their being assigned the task of eliminating the then Chief Minister of Gujarat (Narendra Modi) and another prominent leader of Gujarat (Amit Shah). This part of the Headley testimony was soon available in the public domain.

A vital letter, which was found filed in one of the several litigations in the Jundal case, is the letter of Daniel Clegg, the then Legal Attache in the US Embassy in Delhi. He had expressly assured India of total cooperation of the US government in access to David Headley for questioning.

However, the then Indian government, including I recall, the then Home Minister Sushil Kumar Shinde (2012-2014), pedalled a public lie that the US government had been resisting any further access to David Headley. Often, NIA documentation was offered to the media as proof. Several years later, the then NIA, under the UPA regime, was accused of excising vital portions of the Headley testimony for tendering before the courts. However, the security establishment knew that the NIA had submitted a full 'tour report' containing the full Headley testimony to Home Minister Chidambaram.

---

13 26/11 handler Abu Jundal and others have been found guilty in the 2006 Aurangabad arms haul case by the MCOCA court in Mumbai in 2016.

14 A commando or guerrilla.

A very pertinent point is to what extent was Headley's interrogation excised? By admission, the references to Ishrat Jahan as 'a botched mission' has been revealed in the Abu Jundal trial.

Maybe, the portion defining filmmaker Rahul Bhatt's role in assisting David Headley in carrying out the recce of the Taj and Trident Hotels in 26 November 2008 too was excised for the courts. *The nation wants to know how is it that a person who accompanies Headley on a recce—takes detailed rounds of Mumbai city—claims innocence, saying that he was not aware of what Headley was up to?*

Also why should Rahul's father[15] pedal influence and write to the Union Home Minister? Since the son was innocent and had no idea of what Headley, his companion, was up to, they could have consulted a lawyer, got a statement recorded with any judicial authority under relevant sections of the Criminal Procedure Code and got him exonerated in the public eye.

One more important aspect of Headley's statement was the 'Kasab tradeoff'. In the statement before the trial court in the Abu Jundal case, Headley had reportedly hinted that there were attempts to take hostage some persons— possibly a Director-level person/s from India's security establishments—to be traded off with Ajmal Kasab by the ISI. This testimony was also a part of Headley's NIA interrogation which got edited out from official records.

Attempts to take hostage some Israelis and trade them for Ajmal Kasab's release was revealed in Headley's statement before the court in the Jundal case in March 2016.

However, way back in 2009, immediately after the 26/11 Mumbai attacks, there were whispers amongst the security and intelligence community that there would be attempts to take Indian government officials hostage and trade them off for Ajmal

15 Film-maker Mahesh Bhatt

Kasab's release. This was a purely internal security assessment about Indian officials. People like P K Mishra, then Director (IS), were on high alert, moving about within Delhi police cover. The NIA was very much aware of this. *Was there a line of questioning by the NIA team which interrogated Headley in Chicago in 2009? What was the specific line of questioning? Was there any input from the interrogation with Headley on a possible tradeoff? Was it also part of the answers which were excised?*

For purely public consumption, most of the 'dossier diplomacy' started only after 7 January 2009. Before that, possibly, I was one of the alternative 'target officials' whose 'botched up' attempt to take hostage had already happened. Was some collaboration in existence between some top Indian political entity with Pakistani establishments? Was it a case of overplaying and recalibration? We do not know.

Fallout of Special Secretary's letter to Delhi Police

I HAVE ALREADY told my readers of the intimidation attempt on me on the night of 30.12.2008, when I had gone to the Rashtrapati Bhavan in connection with the Presidential Assent to the two security Bills that were passed by Parliament in December 2008. It may be recalled that an official communication in this regard was sent to Delhi Police Commissioner on the 19 January 2009. The impact of this communication started showing immediately, that is in the third week of January 2009.

On 23 January 2009, I was scheduled to go to Ahmedabad in connection with a meeting with the Central Government Counsel, Hriday Buch. Actually, Harin Raval, the then Assistant Solicitor General, was on holiday abroad and Buch was standing in for him. The case title was *Sardarji Maghanji Vaghela versus Union of India & others*. The petitioner was a victim of the 2002 Gujarat riots.

People living in Delhi know that to travel in Delhi in winter is a challenging task. It was a Friday and I was to take an early afternoon flight to Ahmedabad, so I did not go to office that morning. The decision on my meeting had been taken late in the evening of 22 January 2009. I was not actually dealing with the subject. But those days, the official team in the Internal Security Division under Joint Secretary Diptivilasa was a buoyant group and everyone would offer and was capable of standing in for another. Otherwise, we could not have handled the challenges thrown up, both, professionally and also politically. A junior officer of my colleague who dealt with the subject was to accompany me and bring the relevant papers directly to the airport.

While I was preparing to travel to Ahmedabad, I received a call from a person called Monga, who identified himself as the Station House Officer of the Dwarka Police Station. He wanted me to narrate the entire story of the 30 night to him. I repeated the sequence of events to this alleged policeman, giving him every specific detail. He said he would come and record a statement in this regard. I told him that I had a flight to catch and upon my return, I would sign a statement in this regard.

The litigation in Ahmedabad required me to travel to and fro between Ahmedabad and Delhi up to the 30 February. Then I was busy in the public interest litigation by interest groups in the Bombay High Court in the aftermath of 26.11.2008, which kept me busy up to the 2 week of February 2009. On the personal front, my wife had suffered an ankle injury which too kept me on my toes. As a result, I had little time to follow up on the more personal 30.12.2008 case. No follow-up call had come in the meanwhile.

I am associated with the Sree Vinayaka Mandir located in Sarojini Nagar, New Delhi since childhood. It is a place for recovery and rejuvenation for me. I had also learnt chanting of the Vedas, scriptures and other edicts of my religion at this place. On every second Sunday, there is an elaborate programme known as Mahanyasa Eka Vara Rudrabhishekam which is performed in the temple. Having been trained in this, I also participate in this religious activity as a *ritwik*.[16] The ritual concludes at about 1:30 pm in the afternoon.

After the conclusion of the programme on 13 February afternoon, I dropped my father at my sister-in-law's place, where he was camping at that time. When I reached home around 3:30pm, I received a call from the reception on the internal phone that some police inspector named Khokhar was waiting to meet me. I asked the guard at the reception to send him in.

Khokhar was a very polite man. He too requested a narration of the intimidation incident again. After I narrated the sequence of events all over again to this man, he requested me to accompany him to the places where all the chasing had taken place and re-run the route, so that he could visualise it better. I agreed and accompanied him. The whole route was revisited.

He also conducted an identification parade (known as TIP) of police personnel posted in Sector -16B police post, Dwarka. They were summoned to the DCP's office located in Sector 19, Dwarka. They were all lined up in front of me. I couldn't find the person who had stopped me at the entrance of the Sector -16B police post, Dwaraka and I told Khokhar, I could not do a positive identification. Khokhar insisted that we have tea in his office. I agreed and we went over to his chamber. There he had also called the in-charge of the Sector -16B police post, Dwarka, one sub inspector called Pankaj Singh Mallick.

He also expressed his anguish and regret at what had happened on 30.12.2008. Mallick said that he was at the Post up to 10:30 pm, when he had to go to attend an emergency call. I let the matter rest after that.

---

16 Among Hindus, one who is trained in recitation of vedas in the shruti/smriti traditions of learning.

However, again some time in the second week of March 2008, Mallick approached me. This was a few days before I had to go to Darussalam (Bandar Seri Beghwan), Brunei as member of the Indian team to an Asia-Pacific Group meeting on Combating Financing of Terrorism and Money Laundering. Although, noticeably, the police personnel investigating the intimidation always landed home just about when I was scheduled to travel, at that time, I did not think much of this.

Mallick brought out a sheet of paper, asking for my statement for closure of the case. I was not prepared for this. I said, I needed time to think over the matter. Accordingly, I also sent a mail to my senior officer, telling him of Mallick's visit and his request for closure.

After my return from Brunie, an Assistant Commissioner of Police from the Vigilance Branch of Delhi Police, named Hari Singh, landed up in my office. Again, I had to go through the trauma of narrating the intimidation details, yet another time. The only benefit of the visit in the office was that the MHA Control Room was under my oversight. In this place, there are secluded spaces where one-to-one meetings can be carried out. I took Singh to one such spot and told him all the details. Later, he too wanted a closure statement. This time, I declined, saying that I needed to consult my seniors.

Thereafter, Hari Singh would call me almost daily. He would call me at most awkward hours, some time when I was in the midst of an important meeting, or while driving back from office etc. Once, he voluntarily offered to come to North Block. I had no option but to receive him. Upon meeting, his common refrain was that I should give a statement seeking closure of the case. It was much later that I began to connect the dots. Why the policemen always came when I was very busy?

The policemen were all under pressure to get closure in the intimidation case. Much later, I asked Hari Singh, were his orders from the officers inside of MHA? He hinted, '*us se oopar*', meaning higher than the MHA officers. Which is the Home Minister. The ground under my feet slipped. But I was still not aware of the entire story, what was actually behind the attack on me?

This case took its first casualty, Sub Inspector Mallick's promotion had been withheld. Vigilance cases had been slapped against him. For what? For failing to secure closure in my case? I agreed to sign a statement for closure of the case with ACP Hari Singh as I did not want to jeopardise the lives and careers of police officers. They would have been unnecessarily victimised, if I had remained adamant. My statement for closure of the case resulted in immediate clearance of Pankaj Singh Mallick from the Vigilance angle and he got his promotion.

But the biggest revelation came a few days later.

Suspicions strengthened

We were gathering for a meeting in the OPS room. The OPS Room is an ante room to the MHA Control Room which is under the domain of Internal Security Division. Whenever the main committee room, Room No.119, was not available, we used to convene our meetings in the OPS room. One of the participants in the meeting very casually said that the 30.12.2008 incident was designed and directed at a political level. One of the agenda was to take 'an officer' of the MHA, someone who would be very vulnerable as hostage, and could be traded with Ajmal Kasab. This cursory remark was most unbelievable, like something out of fiction and not fact. I was too shocked to respond.

At that time, I held back this information from my spouse, family members, colleagues and others. The Delhi Police can corroborate the facts with the relevant records in their possession if at all they have been retained. Delhi Police personnel below the

ACP level have to maintain diaries as per laid-down procedure.

Till the failure to kidnap me, that is from 27.11.2008 to 30.12.2008, for 33 days, the Pakistani establishment had maintained an ambivalent position on the 26/11 Mumbai attacks. They refused to admit Kasab was a Pakistani citizen. It took another week after the 'botched last ditch effort to kidnap an Indian official' for Pakistan to acknowledge the Mumbai carnage. Only on 7 January 2009 did any response accepting involvement of Pakistanis was first accepted by Pakistan.

I had sensed the conspiracy. Now at last I began to understand the plot. There was some support from the Indian side for the narrative that Pakistan was *not involved* in the 26/11 Mumbai carnage. Also to the narrative perhaps that Kasab could not be interrogated as he had to be allowed to go free, in exchange for an Indian official, a narrative akin to the 1999 IC 814 one.

I do not want to hazard a guess on which political entity had designed the 2008 intimidation script. I also do not want to hazard any guess as to what was the reason for this. It is a fact that I had been subject to an unfortunate experience in the middle of the night, when I was out on official work. I had heard it from one of the security agencies, the reason was political. Also there was pressure on the policemen to close the case arising out of the MHA protest. However, after a decade, the question that troubles me is, had they succeeded, would the narrative have changed? We do not know. Maybe, a colour might have been assigned to this attack on me, like in the Samjhauta Blasts.

In this context, the dossier of the Ministry of External Affairs relating to Ajmal Kasab's nationality may be of interest to readers.

Reference to a telephone call between the then External Affairs Minister Pranab Mukherjee and the then Pakistani President had got included in the dossier on 26.11.2008 handed over by Pakistan to India. To rebut Pakistan's claim about Mukherjee (India's President till 2017)—that he had called Zardari on 26.11.2008—this could have been easily done with electronic evidence. Mukherjee said a 'hoax call' report was planted in the Pak dossier. Interestingly, the MEA chose to textually rebut it. Further, what material evidentiary value did this Pak dossier serve in the investigation into the Mumbai attacks is not clear. (See page 220)

NAC members tried to save Kasab

Aruna Roy, Harsh Mander among 203 sought mercy for 26/11 terrorist

KUMAR CHELLAPPAN/ANNAPURNA JHA ■ CHENNAI/NEW DELHI

A serving member and a former member in the Sonia Gandhi-headed National Advisory Council (NAC) were among the 203 peti-

revealed that Aruna Roy, who is at present a member of the influential NAC, and Harsh Mander, a former member in the body, were among the scores of others, including several journalists and social activists who filed mercy pleas for Kasab.

"Mander, a former NAC member, wrote to the President of India seeking clemency for Ajmal Kasab, who had been sentenced to death by a trial court as well as the Supreme Court. But President Pranab Mukherjee was gracious enough to reject the clemency petition as well as the strong rec-

Swamy distributed copies of the letter received under the Right to Information Act by one of his party members about details of persons who sent in mercy petitions to the President for Kasab. Both Roy and Mander figure in the 203-strong list.

Besides the two, another key social activist figuring in the list happens to be Nikhil Dey. "These are the kind of people sitting as members of the NAC to decide the fate of this country," Swamy alleged.

Mander, who was a member of the NAC till last year, had also courted controversy for his pleas to save Afzal Guru, one of the main

Mander sent an article, 'The Quality of Mercy', that he had written after Kasab's hanging in November last year saying it reflected his views on the issue. "I feel even more worried when the Supreme Court declares in a particular matter of a political crime of terror that the death sentence must be applied to 'satisfy the collective conscience' of the nation; or the clearly political motivations in the haste with which Kasab was executed," Mander said in the article.

He, however, admitted that Kasab's "trial was fair, his conviction just, his crime merciless and horrendous therefore many celebrated his hanging as fitting closure to a

HEADLEY EYED SIDDHIVINAYAK, BARC

RECCE OF TARGETS IN MUMBAI FOR ATTACK

David Headley visited Mumbai seven times beginning September 2006 till the November 2008 attacks for a reconnaissance of targets

➤ **He flew in to Mumbai from Karachi six times, on:** Sept 14, 2006 | Feb 22, 2007 | March 26, 2007 | Sept 4, 2007 | April 9, 2008

From Lahore once, on | July 1, 2008

From Abu Dhabi once, on an unknown date

" CST was not surveyed as a target. But for people who came, for them to leave

I was assigned the task to conduct reconnaissance of Taj Mahal Hotel. A mock-up of Taj was also prepared. I made a surveillance video of the conference room on the second floor

PLACES SURVEYED

➤ **Taj Mahal Hotel,** Colaba

➤ **Bhagat Singh Marg,** Colaba, where Leopold Café is situated. Headley made a video of the entire road. Landmarks in Colaba were surveyed, including **Chabad House**

➤ **Trident Hotel,** Nariman Point

➤ **Siddhivinayak Temple,** Prabhadevi

IDENTIFIED AS TARGETS

➤ All surveyed places except Siddhivinayak temple

➤ Naval air station, state police HQ and **BARC** were spared by 26/11 attackers

The 26/11 terror attacks in Mumbai left as many as 166 people dead; the terrorists ravaged several places in the city — Hotel Taj (below), the Chhatrapati Shivaji Terminus (above), Leopold Cafe, Oberoi Trident hotel, Cama Hospital & Nariman House. Ajmal Kasab (left) was the lone attacker who was arrested. He was hanged in India in November 2012.

UGLY FACES OF TERROR

HAFIZ MOHD SAEED

Lashkar-e-Taiba founder Hafiz Mohammad Saeed (left) continues to move around openly across Pakistan despite a bounty of $10 million (₹60 crore approx.) on him announced by the US. Though the US and the UN have declared Saeed's Jamaat-ud-Dawa a front for the LeT, Pakistani authorities have not banned the JuD and have only placed the group on a "watch list" maintained under the Anti-Terrorism Act.

ZAKIUR REHMAN LAKHVI

LeT commander Zakiur Rehman Lakhvi was arrested during a raid on a camp of the banned terror group on the outskirts of Muzaffarabad, the capital of Pakistan-occupied Kashmir, weeks after the Mumbai attacks. Despite being held in the high-security Adiala Jail in Rawalpindi, he continues to direct the activities of the LeT, according to bomb-maker Abdul Karim Tunda, who was recently arrested by Indian authorities.

OTHERS

The other Pakistani accused in the Mumbai attacks are Hammad Amin Sadiq, Mazhar Iqbal alias Abu al-Qama, Abdul Wajid alias Zarrar Shah, Shahid Jamil Riaz (all members of LeT), Jamil Ahmad and Younas Anjum (financiers of the Mumbai attacks).

OFFICE OF THE DY.COMMISSIONER OF POLICE: VIGILANCE
DELHI.

F.No.24 (176) 20290 /HA-MHA/VIG,dated, New Delhi, the 18/6/09.

To

Shri Raman Srivastava,
Special Secretary,
(Internal Security)
Ministry of Home Affairs,
New Delhi.

Subject:- Regarding complaint Shri R.V.S. Mani, Under Secretary(Internal Security), MHA, New Delhi.

Sir,

Kindly refer to your office D.O. letter No.11034/27/2008-IS.VI dt. 19.1.2009. on the subject cited above.

It has been alleged that on the night of 30.12.2008 at about 11.30 P.M. Shri R.V.S Mani, Under Secretary (Internal Security, MHA was chased by four persons on two motorcycles who attempted to waylay him. Shri Mani sought the assistance from police personnel of Police Post Dwarka Sector-13B who appeared to be well acquainted with the stalkers. They insulted and abused him. He was unduly harassed and one baton was allegedly given on his leg and his mobile was also pushed away. The police personnel have also snatched his two Rs.500/- currency notes and other smaller denomination currency notes and threw his wallet for him to pick up.

During enquiry the staff of Police Post 16B Dwarka (there is no Police Post in Sector 13B) have been examined. They denied occurrence of any such incident in the area of police post. They also furnished a copy of Daily Diary of 30.12.2008. On scrutiny of Daily Diary no such DD entry has been found to be lodged. The staff examined included SI Pankaj Malik (I/C PP Sector-16B Dwarka), ASI Umed Singh NO.3051/SW, Const. Bhim Singh NO.1834/SW, Const. Surender NO.713/SW i.e the staff deployed on the intervening night of 30/31.12.2008 as per duty roster.

Shri R.V.S. Mani was requested to identify the alleged police staff since no lead was forth coming. The whole staff posted in Police Post 16B Dwarka were paraded before Shri R.V.S. Mani on the terrace of office of DCP/South-West Distt., Sector-19, Dwarka on 8.2.09. Shri R.V.S. Mani was pretty sure that none of the staff present was involved. Shri Mani has also appraised the features of the persons involved. The PCR staff posted at Z-72 PCR van which has its base in proximity to the Police Post was also examined. They have denied being involved in the incident or knowing anything. Identification of these three police personnel could not be made since it is not alleged that there was any PCR van at the place of occurrence. Three PCR personnel were attending a call at the relevant time at Village Kakrola.

As per duty roster, on 30.12.2008 ASI Umed Singh, HC Krishan Pal NO.457/SW and Const. Rajesh were on emergency duty from 8.00 P.M. To 8.00 A.M. ASI Umed Singh was also doubling up on Motorcycle patrolling with Const. Surender on Anti-snatching picket duty with Const. Sat Narain, NO.1581/SW, Const. Rajesh was on accused duty with Const. Bhim Singh. The staff was deployed on many duties at the same time.

As per per Daily Diary of 30.12.2008 SI Pankaj Malik (I/C Police Post) had arrived from picket duty alongwith staff at 11.15 P.M and gone home. ASI Umed Singh had left the Police Post with Const. Rajesh Kumar to attend a call at 9.00 PM and 03 other calls were also marked to him. The ASI came back to the Police Post at 11.45 P.M. along with Constable after attending the calls. This proves that the ASI was present in the Police Post about 15 minutes after the time of incident. There is no DD entry pertaining to the above incident. Constable Jaivir No.2715/SW had proceeded on patrolling at 11.20 P.M. And he came back at 6.10 A.M. On 31.12.2008. In these circumstances only Constable Bhim Singh No.1834/SW was present at the actual time of incident. However, an explanation of SI Pankaj Malik (I/C Police Post Sector-16B, Dwarka) has been called for lack of supervision on his part and ASI Umed Singh, Constables Rajesh, Bhim Singh, Jaibir Singh, Surinder have been shifted from Police Post, Sector-16B, Dwarka.

Yours faithfully,

DEPUTY COMMISSIONER OF POLICE,
VIGILANCE, NEW DELHI

The colour saffron

FOR THE INTERNAL Security Division, 2009 was relatively a peaceful year. 2008 had been unduly clogged, with excessive pressures both foreseen and unforeseen.

In April 2008, we were busy managing the Olympic torch journey through India by coordinating the security paraphernalia. This had a personal spinoff for me. I had been a candidate for the Kailash Mansarover Yatra as a Liaison Officer. The interview for it was also scheduled in April 2008. The selection was to be done by a group of officers led by Vijay Keshav Gokhale, then Joint Secretary (China), in the Ministry of External Affairs. He was also the officer coordinating the Olympic Torch passage for the Beijing Olympics 2008. He had exposure to my personal performance in the task of coordinating the Olympics Torch passage and this helped in my selection as the Liaison Officer for the Mansarovar Yatra that year. That year, I also got medals in the Delhi State Veteran Athletics Championship in 5km walking and shot put.

It was a time when every one-and-a half months, India faced a terrorist attack in some part of the country. There was also public outcry after 26.11.2008. There was a concerted attempt to colour every one of these attacks as 'saffron', except that it did not succeed in the case of the 26.11.2008 Mumbai attacks.

Presumably, the government of the day also felt that they had overplayed the saffron narrative and some of the attacks were truly preempted. Hence we felt relieved that in spite of being an election year (2009) the challenges on counter-terrorism front were relatively lesser than the year before.

One thing I would like to state here. Many of my esteemed colleagues from the bureaucracy agree that no officer will knowingly place any information which is not a truth in response to a query by a Parliamentarian. This may be in response to a question, or calling attention motion, or special mention or whatsoever. But lying to any House of Parliament is attendant with grave circumstances. Noticeably, during the period when the 'Saffron Terror' narrative was being peddled by the government in power, there was not a single response to any question raised in Parliament in both the Houses, where a reference to Hindu Terror had been made. The responses were primarily as follows:

> Pakistan/PoK-based ISI sponsored groups are/have been found responsible for——so & so terror attack.

Throughout this period, for question after question, this had been the standard response from the government.

The Agencies—the police forces, the security agencies and every institution in the security and law enforcing setup of the country—had said, 'any dialogue with Pakistan was a farce and an exercise in futility'. However, we did have certain interest groups who were able to prevail over the then government.

Since Home Secretary Level Talks 2008 had been rendered

useless, the Agencies had been sceptical about a proposed exchange visit by Judicial Committees (refer to Joint Statement at the end of HSLT 2008) from the two countries. The end result was that the Pakistani Committee visited our prisons while reciprocal Indian request was declined.

Being an election year, another new scheme was also introduced. This was known as 'compensation for victims of terror attacks and communal riots'. It was handled by the National Integration and Human Rights Division. Naturally, the very fact that it was assigned to this Division makes it evident that it was a political largesse intended for the benefit predominantly of victims of communal violence, as it panned out later.

However, the status of investigation of all terror attacks was being monitored by the MHA on a monthly basis. Officials in the the Internal Security Division could clearly see from the documents coming to us, how slowly but surely, the information based on preliminary findings we had from the primary respondents—that is the local police—for every case was changing, changing its original 'status'.

Cases which had been assigned to NIA had their facts turned upside down. Later on in the year, this monthly MHA monitoring and updating exercise came almost to a standstill.

Intelligence since 2005

In 2005, two special groups had been constituted in MHA to be led by the Internal Security Division. One was a cell to monitor the flow of funds to terrorist, FICN trafficking etc. The second was a group to monitor growth of Mosques and Madarsas on both sides of the Indo-Bangladesh and Indo-Nepal Border and flow of funds to these institutions. These groups used to meet regularly.

A very vital and important fact is that all the inputs that MHA had on this were from only Central Agencies. The bordering State governments of those times were fully aware of these activities and the MHA monitoring but were not reporting any information to the Centre.

On the Indo-Bangladesh Border, what was happening in the border districts of West Bengal was rampant radicalisation by Tablighi Jamaat and Harkat-ul-Jihad-al-Islami (HuJI) Bangladesh. The BSF Intelligence had done an excellent job of collecting and collating detailed information at that time. Inputs were being received from the IB too. At certain times, papers from one Joint Intelligence Committee headed by S D Pradhan and later, by H Upadhyay were also regularly corroborating these inputs and emphasising on action. But the then Left government of West Bengal turned blind eye to the growth of this fundamentalism. Also, the periodical WB Governors' Report of the time to the Home Ministry (copy may be available in CS-VI Section) never mentioned the growth of fundamentalist groups even once. The then Governor was Gopalkrishna Gandhi.

This is very relevant now because, had the preemptive action suggested by security agencies been taken by the political establishments in power those days, maybe we could have avoided incidents like in Basirhat, or the reported arms trafficking in Bardhaman etc. It was just a matter of time when such similar incidents occurred in Murshidabad, Cooch Behar and Malda.

On the Indo-Nepal border also, the growth of fundamentalist organisations was very high in Bihar and certain districts of Uttar Pradesh. The flow of funds to these institutions were from Saudi Arabia, Kuwait through hawala channels and Nepal. Certain Pakistani (if I remember correctly Karachi-based call girls also being sent as honey traps to entice Indian officers) women were used as couriers. In one incident, an officer of the FCRA Division, who had gone on a routine inspection in Bihar, was attacked because he had dared to seek inspection of a NGO which was running a Madrasa. This NGO actually belonged to Mohammad Shahabuddin, now doing time in jail.

In so far as Mumbai 26/11 was concerned, it was not to be monitored in the regular forum. A special team of two officers of the level of Joint Secretary—one from the Ministry of Home Affairs (Secretariat) and another from an investigative agency—was constituted. They received the evidences collected by the State police through the State government, examined their efficacy and took it to the Home Minister. Whether the Special Secretary and Home Secretary were kept in the loop or not is not known to me. The team used men from Internal Security on a need basis. Otherwise the two officers did their job on their own.

Terror Funding

One very important achievement of the team of that time needs to be highlighted. Financial Action Task Force (FATF) is a global cooperative institutional mechanism for combating laundering of money and financing of terrorism under the aegis of the United Nations. At that time, India was attempting to get membership of this body.

The entitlement for membership required a minimum of compliance, with 6-9 out of 40 high standard benchmarks for anti-money laundering and 9 for combating terror financing, known as Recommendations and Special Recommendations. These benchmarks pertained to legal frameworks, implementation of these legal frameworks, the MIS on implementation etc. Suffice it to say here that eventually when India got the membership, it was on account of most of the recommendations pertaining to the Ministry of Home Affairs which were found compliant to these benchmarks to qualify for the membership.

The domain areas of other ministries/departments including the Department of Revenue and Department of Economic Affairs were found wanting in meeting these compliance requirements. I am given to understand that these benchmarks have now been modified. One of the salient persons to whom this success is attributable is P K Mishra, then Director (Internal Security). This gentleman was an Income Tax Service officer. Along with his exposure to counter-terrorism, he had expertise in putting the compliance requirements in place in respect of the MHA domain. In the process, in the government we had an officer who had this unique competency to really attack terror funding legally and administratively. In addition to this international membership, the MHA team also had a lot more going on in the international arena.

It is well acknowledged that finance is the lifeline of terrorism. It is a fact that Indian intelligence agencies and revenue agencies have busted a lot of cases of funding of terror in India.

In reply to a Rajya Sabha starred question no. 136, for answer on 07.03.2007 regarding funding routes of terrorists to questions from MPs Syed Azeez Pasha (CPM) and K E Ismail (CPI), the documents presented revealed:

> According to available reports, terrorist groups in India are receiving funds from abroad mainly through hawala and informal channels. Flow of funds to terrorist groups is estimated to be of the order of several crores every year, though the exact quantum of funds being received by them is difficult to estimate.
>
> Funding of Jehadi Groups:
>
> Flow of funds to terrorist outfits including LeT, JeM, HuM and others is estimated to be of the order of several crores every year, though the exact quantum of funds being received by them is difficult to estimate. Of late, financing of terrorist groups has become systematic and organized. Two trends are noticeable: first, it is now institutionalized and secondly, it has acquired global dimension. The transfer system has become highly sophisticated and is also based on manipulation of formal channels.

Major sources of funding as per the then available inputs were as follows:

Direct financial assistance from ISI is estimated at Rs. 84 crore annually. Overall, the Pak establishment/ Pak ISI is reported to be spending Rs. 300-400 crore annually to sponsor terrorism in India.

FICN is also given to terrorists, which is mainly routed via Nepal. Inputs suggest involvement of Pak diplomatic mission at Kathmandu.

Reports suggest that drug money is also being used by jehadi groups. No authentic estimates are however available on the amount. It is also noted by agencies that the jehadi groups in association with smugglers could also be earning money through the drug trade. According to Defence Intelligence Agency (DIA) estimates, at least 15% of Pak funding comes from drug money. In Afghanistan, net opium cultivation climbed by 64% since 2002, and total 'export value' to neighbours increased by 22%. (i.e. US $ 2.3 bn. to $ 2.8 bn.) Trafficking profits also increased from $ 1.3 bn to 2.2 bn.

Donations are also being collected by Jehadi groups directly. Jehadi outfits also launch fund raising campaigns in Pakistan to support their activities (*The Herald*, July , 2005). Mosque collections and Zakat are also used by jehadi groups. They are also reported to be using money earned by the sale of skins of goats slaughtered on festivals. No estimates are available on this source.

Pan Islamic Charity Organisations continue to offer funds. Major such organisations are International Islamic Relief Organisation (IIRO), Iqra Charitable Institution, Rabita al Alam al Islami, World Assembly of Muslim Youth (WAMY) and Al Rashid Trust. IIRO has also set up Sanabil Al Khair Foundation (SAKF) at Jeddah to streamline fund flows. Funds collected by the SAKF are largely managed by Habib Bank Ltd., located at Islamabad. Some of the other institutions registered abroad include the Madni Trust (UK) of the HUJI, AL Haramain (Oregon), Global Relief Foundation (London), Islamic Relief Worldwide (Burbank), Kashmir

Relief Fund (Canada), Umma Relief International (Saudi Arabia), Servants of Suffering Humanity (South Africa) and others... according to the details available at that time of the break up of terrorist funding.

The broad estimates are as follows:

25% comes from Pakistan; 15% comes from narcotics; 10% from arms sale; 10% from FICN; 10% from zakat; 20% from donations received; and the last 10% from extortion.

The Harkat-ul-Mujahideen has declared an increase in its annual income from Rs. 25.067 crore in 2003 to Rs. 30.26 crore in 2004, 66.3% expenditure was incurred on field operations, and balance on 'base camps'. Expenditure on training showed an increase from Rs. 1.55 crore in 2003 to Rs. 2.2 crore in 2004 suggesting an increase in the cadre strength. This is only declared budget of HuM. The quantum of hidden budget is not available. Figures for other terrorist groups are not available. LeT gets priority in funding (60% according to some estimates). Sayed Salahuddin, Hizbul Mujahideen (HM) Supreme Commander was being paid approx. Rs. 1.7 crore per month by ISI in 2007.

Channels of funding which were identified in 2001-2007 are as follows:

Hawala routes going into Delhi, Mumbai, Lucknow, Jaipur, Bangalore and Kerala (Hezb-e-Islami module arrested May 28, 2005 in New Delhi). Dubai and Singapore are reported to be important hawala centres. Dawood Ibrahim's network is also being used to send funds through this channel.

Regular banking channels (e.g. Habib Bank (Pak) which has links with Himalayan Bank (Nepal JV). The Himalayan Bank branches along the Indo-Nepal border are reported to be providing funds to terrorists in Nepal.

Personal visits (cash):

Pak High Commission (e.g. Sheikh Abdul Aziz (APHC-G) was arrested (February 17, 2004 in New Delhi) when he came out of the Pak High Commission (PHC) with 94,000

Dirhams and Rs. 1 lakh in FICN).

The Credit/debit cards issued by Muslim Commercial Bank, which has a tie up with international financial/commercial companies such as 'Master/Visa have also come to adverse notice.

Prominent illustrative examples of the period are:

An instance of the Pak mission in Delhi providing cash for militancy was witnessed in the arrest of Ms Anjum Zamruda Habib of the Muslim Khawateen Markaz who was apprehended (February 6, 2003) after she had received Rs. 3.3 lakhs from the Pakistan High Commission in Delhi and was carrying the cash on her person with instructions to pass on the money to terrorist outfits.

Mujib Nabi Ahmed, a Pak resident agent was arrested from Jamnagar, Gujarat on February 28, 2003 while communicating sensitive defence related information about Army units located at Pune and Ahmed Nagar from a Cyber Café at Jamnagar through e-mail. A note pad recovered from him contained detail account of payments amounting to Rs. 1,58,000/- received through hawala from the Karachi based Pakistan Intelligence Operative (PIO), Lt. Col. Omar between May, 2002 and February, 2003.

Masood Akhtar, a Pak resident agent arrested from Hissar by Haryana Police on March 26, 2003 admitted to have been receiving payments from his handlers in Pakistan through a Mumbai operated Hawala channel.

One Altaf Hussain Mir, a resident of Srinagar, was taken into custody on April 5, 2003 after a sum of Rs. 93 lakh was recovered from him. Mir was working as the financial point man for Saiful Islam (late Chief of the J&K division of the HM). A diary found in Mir's possession revealed the occurrence of financial transactions on behalf of the HM, to the tune of Rs. 3.5 crore.

In the course of Army operations (April 2003) in the Hill Kaka area of J&K, diaries were recovered that showed the receipt of nearly Rs. 67 lakhs by the slain militants from as many as 18 terrorist tanzeems.

On the 10.05.2003, a Hizbul Mujahideen militant namely Ghulam Mohiudden Bhat, was arrested by Delhi Police with Rs. 6.5 Lakh along with a Chinese pistol and 16 live cartridges etc.

May 13, 2003: Zafar Umar Khan, son of Mohd. Sadique Khan, resident of Poonch (J&K) was arrested by Delhi Police when in addition to arms and ammunition Rs. 4 lakhs hawala money was recovered.

On August 8, 2003 Mohd. Masood @ Mustafa, a UDC in Pak Embassy, Kathmandu was caught red handed by Nepal Police trying to sell fake Indian currency worth Rs. 45,000/-. He was arrested, detained and a FIR was lodged against him.

On August 28, 2003, one Noor Mohammad Tantray @ Peer Baba@ Gulzar Ahmed Bhat@ Ulwais along with his associates was apprehended by Delhi Police along with Rs. 85, 000/- and grenade launcher, grenade shells, hand grenades, electronic detonators etc. Further investigation led to the recovery of Rs. 19.20 Lakh.

December 7, 2003: Tarif Hussain son of Bashir Hussain, resident of district Rajouri and Tanzeem Ahmed of Thana Mandi, Rajouri, 2 militants of Hiz-bul-Mujahiddin (HM) were apprehended in Delhi. On search 2 AK 56 rifles with 120 rounds, 4.3 kg of RDX amongst others, 15 lakhs hawala money were recovered.

On January 22, 2004 Ayaz Ahmed Shah @ Iqbal belonging to a Pak based terrorist organization was arrested by Delhi Police with 3.5 kgs explosive and Rs. 3 lakhs was recovered from him. Sheikh Abdul Aziz (APHC-G) was arrested on February 17, 2004 in New Delhi, when he came out of the Pak High Commission (PHC) with 94,000 Dirhams and Rs. 1 lakh in FICN.

March 28, 2004: Irshad Ahmed Malik, son of Mohammed Amin Malik of district Doda (J&K) was arrested in Delhi when in addition to arms and ammunition Rs. 2.75 lakhs hawala money was recovered.

On March 5, 2005 Hamid Hussain @ Abu Faisal and

Mohammad Sariq were apprehended by Delhi Police with Rs. 2.5 Lakh Indian currency and Singapore Dollars 10,000 along with one satellite phone, one pistol, live cartridges, hand grenades etc.

On March 25, 2005 Mohammad Ishaq Ittoo was arrested by Delhi Police with Rs. 2.5 lakh of hawala money, 5.5 kgs of RDX, and two electronic detonators.

On August 26, 2005 Aslam Wani of Srinagar was arrested by Delhi Police with Rs. 62.96 lakhs of hawala money along with 5 kgs. of RDX, 10 electronic detonators etc.

On November 11, 2005 Tariq Ahmed Dar, main conspirator, coordinator and financier of LeT was arrested by Delhi Police. He is involved in the Delhi blasts that took place at Sarojini Nagar, Paharganj and Govindpuri on October 29, 2005. He had received Rs. 4.86 lakhs from abroad for executing the blasts.

On February 3, 2006, Nasir Safi Mir, was arrested by Delhi Police with large quantity of explosives, detonator, ABCD timer, arms and ammunitions etc. Rs. 55 lakhs was transferred to India through money exchange companies through hawala channels for terrorist purpose.

On May 8, 2006, two LeT militants, Firoz Abdul Latif Ghaswala and Mohammad Ali Chippa were arrested by Delhi Police along with 4 kgs of RDX, 4 detonators and cash of Rs. 50,000.

On July 10, 2006, Azaj Hussain Khwaja was apprehended by Delhi Police with Rs. 49 lakhs hawala money and 2.050 kgs of RDX.

Habib Bank

In these extracts of replies to Parliamentary questions et al, the role of Habib Bank Limited in terror funding is clear. Habib Bank Limited has a very interesting personal anecdote. There was a proposal from the Reserve Bank of India, received through the Department of Financial Services, Ministry of Finance, for grant of permission to open branches of Habib Bank Limited in India.

Normally, it is well within the domain of RBI or Department of Financial Services. It was a single file proposal meaning, the Department had referred the entire file to us instead of just shooting a letter to MHA seeking our responses. The final concluding note was signed by Arun Ramanathan, the then Secretary of the Department and marked to his counterpart, the then Home Secretary .

I do not remember the date on which the proposal was received. From the Home Secretary's office, in the laid-down format, the file in its downward journey landed on my desk. No sooner had it landed on my desk, I started getting calls for expediting a favourable response from officers in the Department of Financial Services.

An officer, introducing himself as belonging to the office of one Mr Verma, a Joint Secretary, in the Department of Financial Services, started calling me on my landline. When I checked with my counterpart in the Department of Financial Services, he said there are many such wheelerdealers who misuse the names of officers in their Department.

Notwithstanding, I myself had adequate inputs regarding the adversarial activities of the Habib Bank Limited. I also got some additional inputs from our Agencies, recorded all these adverse records and put these up to my seniors for consideration. The result was predictable. But the aftermath was even more. Habib Bank was denied permission to open branches in India.

The whispering rooms

INDIA IS A country where things unsaid speak volumes. Though not on any official document, one gets to hear things as an MHA official. Actually, it is not as if just one person gets to know, many in the ministries and government get to know what is happening, at any given point in time. Of course, there were the usual office gossips about transfers, punishments etc. Apart from this there were rumours of a more serious nature.

There were some whispers shared in the periodical meetings of the Special Economic Intelligence Cell that the highest office in the country was not happy about the MHA's role in stopping Habib Bank.

I have already said earlier that in November 2007, the United Nations Counter Terrorism Executive Directorate visited India. They had come to assess the level of preparedness and systems in place in India to face and counter terror attacks. Their mandate was derived from several of the resolutions passed in the United Nations Security Council.

Their report was generally appreciative of the Indian infrastructure and systems in place. Note: This was just a year before the 26/11 attacks. They did in their report recommend certain steps. But these were in the form of reinforcements and higher level of iteration. The relevance of my discussing this report is to share the fact that in India, the framework and infrastructure were in place and had been acknowledged by the United Nations more than a year before 26/11. The human resources were there too. However, in 2008, terror attacks continued to happen. Why? Let me tell you another story.

The D Gang's long arm

A senior Indian Foreign Service Officer, H S Puri, was to take up appointment as the Permanent Representative of India to the United Nations in 2009. While doing his preparatory work, he had identified that the United States as well the United Nations were attempting to include Dawood Ibrahim in the United Nations Security Council Resolution 1267 List. This would have proscribed the man's cross-country travels, cross-country money transaction, cross-country movement of arms etc.

At first, this officer sought written information from the R&AW and MHA on Dawood. Ministry of Home Affairs is not the repository of information and hence we requested our agencies and CBI to collect and collate whatever information was available on Dawood. While the agencies are intelligence gathering agencies, what was required to buttress the case in the United Nations was more of evidentiary nature.

Only CBI could give such information of evidentiary nature, the backup evidence was all with them. But no response to Puri's query came forth from the CBI, India's premier investigative agency in 2009, when P Chidambaram was Home Minister.

Puri later convened a meeting in his chamber. I attended the meeting in which officers of MHA agencies as well as Ministry of External Affairs territorial divisions were present. However, no one ever came from the CBI. CBI, which always claimed to have mountain of evidence against Dawood, was clearly desisting from sharing this information with the nation's nominated Permanent Representative to the UN.

Whispers. I repeat whispers led to the information that some political quarters were against providing any hardcore evidence against Dawood, to the UN.

At that time, I did not believe this as truth. I also do not know whether the CBI later shared this evidence with the Permanent Representative. As is the laid-down procedure, MHA kept on writing to CBI, as they say in government parlance, we kept sending CBI 'reminders'. Much later, I was to realise that the CBI was amenable to accommodating political narratives.

Opportunity Costs

Reginald Revans was a great management thinker. He started his career as a nuclear scientist. He was perturbed by the results of research and hence started asking questions. This process of asking questions became the theme of the theory propounded by him. Revans became an organisational thinker and one of his greatest books is titled, *Action Learning*. In 1994, I had the opportunity of meeting him at his residence in Altrincham in Lancashire County in the UK. He gave me a signed copy of his book. It is a treasure I still hold dear. But more importantly, his ideology is more relevant.

The very essence of his thinking is, every participant should ask the right questions for any organisation to be a learning, developing and enriching organisation. This inculcated in me the urge to raise questions. If not before anyone else, to myself and thus increase my own knowledge.

In this process two things that keep agitating me: while after every unfortunate terror attack the casualties are counted in numbers—of deaths, injuries, security forces killed etc.—no one has ever assessed the loss of assets, both hard and soft.

At the start of my career I cut my teeth in the Industry Ministry. Those days it was called the Department of Industrial Development. Hence, I am curious to know how terrorist disturbances affect industrial activity as well as productivity and what is its overall impact on the Indian economy? Once when I was reading the story of a survivor of the Mumbai train attacks, I learnt that prior to the attack, the survivor was a biotechnologist working on frontier areas of research. But the attack crippled him. Unfortunately, it may be a personal loss, yet it should also be appreciated that it is indeed a loss of critical human resource to the nation.

In this context, movement of a consignment between Delhi to Mumbai in my days in the Industry Ministry could take any time between 20 to 30 days. Hence the Udyog Bhavan was flooded with gifting liaison officers of various companies chasing files, so that their paperwork for movement of imported capital goods, or export consignments are seamlessly transported. Loss to industrial activity and cascading loss to economy and tax net on account of law and order disturbances are never factored in, in our accounting process for terrorism.

These are only an opportunity cost as an economist put it. But to drive away investments on account of law and order is a crime on the state. This also happened in my tenure in the Internal Security Division. People may recall the Nandigram and Singur disturbances in this context.

In one case, leading automobile manufacturer Tatas had dreamt a people's car which later was brought out as the Nano. They had acquired land for setting up the plant in West Bengal. Along with the Tatas, their ancillary vendors had also bought land and had started fabricating for their respective plants. Leave alone any loss of land, this plant along with its suppliers chain, would have brought direct employment opportunities to so many locals.

But Mamata Banerjee, a prominent political leader of West Bengal, scuttled the project. This leader mobilised the masses. A challenging law and order situation was created. As a result, huge resource deployment had to be done, causing pressure on the forces. The cost of this will never be factored. But the investments on account of both Singur and Nandigram were driven out. Two huge investment opportunities lost to Bengal. The locals lost job opportunities. The automobile investor shifted to Gujarat, with a resultant rise in the cost of the project. The wasted resources went down the drain. The investor had to suffer time lag in the project. Is there any compensation from the protestors?

But the irony hasn't stopped. This political leader was elected the next Chief Minister of the State. I generally tend to agree with Bibek Debroy of NITI Ayog on the demographic dividend. But this dividend can be harnessed only if these are invested upon by way of skills and also offered opportunity. Otherwise, such huge cache of youth idle, with no opportunity for productive deployment, is a bombshell of social catastrophe waiting to happen. It is like sitting on a volcano. That's one of the aggregators of today's problem in that State with terrorist incidents like Basirhat, Bardhaman etc.

The Bunty-Babli cases

Being a civil servant has the virtue of being exposed to various situations. Sometimes, situations narrated in fictions come true. Many readers might have read the famous novelist Jeffrey Archer's *Honour Among Thieves*. The protagonist was a small-time criminal who makes a living by forging originals. He was hired to and he did forge the American Declaration of Independence. Similarly, we have our own desi version of the Bollywood film, *Bunty aur Babli,* in this the famous Taj Mahal was sold with forged documents.

One late evening on a Saturday, while we were preparing to go home, a telephone call from the PMO stopped us in our tracks. We were told to wait for instructions regarding some matter warranting urgent attention. After a while, an envelope was handed over to Director (Internal Security). Upon opening the envelope, we were astonished. We did not know whether to laugh or cry.

Some iconic property in Lutyens Delhi belonging to the Government of India and the official residence of the incumbent Prime Minister had been sold. The purchaser was an NRI from the UK. He had purchased the property, and the conveyance had been registered in the Amritsar Sub Registrar Office in Punjab. Anyone inquisitive to know may visit the Amritsar Sub Registrar Office and inspect the folios pertaining to the period 2005-2007.

Since his possession was not forthcoming, the NRI initiated court proceedings and got an execution order from a court in the UK. I do not recall if it was the Sheffield Court or the Coventry Court. The said order was served on the Indian High Commission, London, who had passed it on to their Ministry and the Prime Minister's Office.

The Internal Security Division had to do the job of investigation, inquiry, and settlement. In the process, later we were informed that one Assistant Registrar in the land record office was suspended and proceeded against as per the rules.

Who is the victim?

Actually, we as a society, never give credit to policemen when they do an outstanding job. I would like to share with my readers some relevant portions of my draft affidavit which was filed in the Allahabad High Court.

Cooperation between the intelligence agencies of the Central government and the State government of UP has been good, and significant operational successes have been achieved in recent times due to such cooperation. It is worthwhile to mention here that three Pakistani terrorists of a particular terrorist group were arrested in a well-coordinated operation by the UP Police based on information from a Central agency.[17] Similarly, a major tragedy was averted with the busting of a terrorist module, which had plans to target a passenger train during the Shraavan Mela in the month of July. Earlier, the Central government agencies had made important contributions towards successful investigation of major terrorist crimes such as the terrorist attack on Ram Janma Bhoomi at Ayodhya and the twin blasts at Varanasi.

It is not that these were a one-off event. Cooperation between law enforcing and security agencies of Centre and State is a continuous process. We had achieved a lot of success in preventing and preempting many terror attacks which go unreported. I would like to highlight a few attacks which the people should know about. They will respect the police and security establishment. They will stop ridiculing them. It is for a social cause that I am bringing this on record.

A very vital security-related establishment is located in a west coast town named Bhatkal. In very close proximity is a breeding ground for terror activities. One of the prominent leaders of the Indian Mujahideen, Yasin Bhatkal hails from Bhatkal. He has the name of this place as a part of his name. He is serving his term, having been convicted in one of the attacks he had engineered. There are two more, presumably his brothers Riaz and Iqbal, who are also Indian Mujahedeen members, whose names have also prominently figured in terror attacks, terror funding, FICN trafficking etc.

---

17 http://www.thehindu.com/news/national/uttar-pradesh-ats-arrests-suspected-terrorists/article18152357.ece
https://timesofindia.indiatimes.com/india/in-raids-across-3-states-up-cops-bust-let-funding-ring/articleshow/63457859.cms

Sometime ago, a report was received that there was the possibility of poisoning of water supply to a scientists' colony in a security establishment in Bhatkal. The input was shared with security agencies of the concerned State. The Director General of Police of the State, R Srikumar who later on went on to become a statutory functionary as the Vigilance Commissioner with the Central Vigilance Commission, led the initiative to prevent the attack. Very few know about this success story.

Another excellent success story which never got reported is about a report regarding an attempt to cause disturbance in a very historical and prominent mosque, Jama Masjid Delhi, and to create a communal cauldron in the country, this was before 2010.

The local police were informed. A possible attack of a huge magnitude was averted. This apart, the attack had the potential of creating communal disturbances across the country. I congratulate the local police, especially the Inspector General-level officer who led the initiative to preempt this attack.

The reason I want to highlight this is that the designs from Pakistan and PoK do not always target the general populace, the general public in India. They also specifically target Muslims to create a sense of disaffection against their non-Muslim compatriots.

We have to see each incident of this kind in the larger perspective—that the location of the Mosque is surrounded by dense population as well as it is a place of dense traffic with immense parking problems. According to inputs received by the MHA, terrorists had planned to block even the entry/exit to the place of worship by parking vehicles haphazardly and create panic among the faithful on the day of Eid. Then their agents were to provoke the people trapped inside, stating that it was a plan to target those who had assembled there. The place is a very pious place for the believers. Hence the instigation would have had the desired effect.

One important factor has to be stated here. A scheme for compensation for victims of terrorism and communal disturbances had just then been announced. The event would have been a double bonanza for many middle men and self-styled leaders. May be they were salivating at the prospect of a cut from the victims' compensation.

But the larger question is who is a victim of terror attack?

Do the casualties reported and their survivors, the injured only constitute the victim of terror attacks?

Are the security forces who suffer while preempting such attacks not victims? Is Tukaram Omble not one?

Needless to say, there are many others who suffer. Not on the field, but in many other ways. In their desire to serve the nation, to serve humanity, these people suffer. Take the case of Rajinder Kumar and his team members from SIB, Ahmedabad at the time of the Ishrat Jahan crossfire. Or the several police officers of Gujarat—the N K Amins, the Barots etc. Is Col Shrikant Purohit not a victim of terrorism? I have myself been a victim. I have lost my parents when yet some years were left in them, they died worrying about my safety. Am I not a victim of terrorism?

During the years 2008 to 2009, we had also to deal with law and order problems caused on account of the Maharashtra Navnirman Sena's hostility towards migrants from certain parts of India. Close monitoring was launched in order to safeguard the life and property of the victim groups.

The real time problems need to be put in proper perspective here. Here the governments, both at the Centre and the State, were trying to control and safeguard the situation. At the same time, we had the Bihari politician Lalu Prasad, whose people were the target of MNS ire. Lalu Prasad aggravated the problem by announcing that he would perform Chaat Puja in

Mumbai. No political leader would counsel him. The amount of resources that had to be deployed in securing the State and keeping the situation under control after his announcement was another challenge.

Security funding

When the resource deployment on security is concerned, there is a general thinking amongst citizens, and particularly amongst the political class, that it's all being done by the government. Little does anyone realise that the resource availability is finite.

In the same period, we were also confronted with challenging situation on the borders of Haryana and Rajasthan. An ethnic group known as Gujjars was agitating for extension of reservation to them. Internal Security Division's domain is not to go into the merits of their plea. The Gujjar agitation had crippled the border areas. The movement of goods and traffic had come to a halt. Train movements had been halted. If I recall correctly, some of the agitators had camped on the main Delhi-Mumbai rail route. We were very close to deploying the Army for clearing the rail tracks of these agitators. It was one challenge which exposed me to the legal provisions regarding deployment of the Army in such contingent situations.

The Godhra case and other matters

As I have said earlier, 2009 was a relatively comfortable year for us in the Internal Security Division. We were generally going through the motions of monitoring, examining inputs from various agencies. Even going through the motions in the IS Division was quite a challenging task, especially with the Control Room under my oversight.

The officers of the Control Room every day dished out the latest security contingencies from all over the country. This could relate to skirmish in the North East, a disturbance in

J&K, a problem in Naxal-affected areas or even a communal disturbance. The menu in a vast land like India with its infinite complexities was varied.

It was for the respective functional Divisions to calibrate and respond but the MHA IS Division was involved because of the oversight of the Control Room. That year, we had also convened two Chief Minister's Conferences, one on 7.1.2009 and another on 17.7.2009.

The first one was a political statement by the then Home Minister. I was mostly away on a task in Karnataka and had little involvement in it. Also based on the reports/record of the proceedings it seemed to be an exercise in reinventing the wheel.

In the meanwhile, I got involved in the case filed by Sardarji Maghanji Vaghela who was a kin of a victim of the 2002 Godhra train burning. At this time, I also got to know some salient facts which are part of the first-level investigation.

It transpired that in the Aman Guest House opposite to the Godhra Railway Station, owned by one Haji Sahib who got acquitted in the case, 140 litres of petrol had been stored for carrying out this carnage. The relief petition was in the Gujarat High Court. The petitioner sought justice for the victims of terrorism and also prosecution of perpetrators under the then POTA. From the Internal Security Division, I had been asked to deal with this case.

In this context, it came to my knowledge that while repealing POTA and incorporating some of its provisions in the Unlawful Activities (Prevention) Act, amended in 2004, some saving clause in POTA had been used to constitute several POTA Review Committees for several States.

One such committee was constituted for going into cases relating the State of Gujarat on 2.11.2004. This panel gave a clean chit to some of the perpetrators of the Godhra carnage.

As I told you earlier, the case had come up first on 27.1.2009 before the Gujarat High Court, soon after I was intimidated on a cold winter night. I went to Ahmedabad on 23.1.2009, got a draft of the Union of India' s position done in consultation with Hriday Buch, who was standing in for ASG Raval, at Ahmedabad.

Some facts as brought to my knowledge from records while handling this case are recalled below:

> ...that while supporting the case of the petitioner, the State Government has chosen to read the statements of few of the witnesses which finds place in the paper book at pages 278, 225 to 235 (Jabir Binyamin page 278, Shaukat @ Bano page 227, Salim @ Salman page 229/235).
>
> ...the material collected during the course of investigation is taken at its face value, it reveals that Sabarmati Express reached Godhra on 28.02.2002 at 7:43 am It had 18 coaches as it is borne out from the statement of on duty Guard Shri Satyanarayan Verma. Out of the said 18 coaches, there were 10 reserved coaches, 6 general coaches and 2 coaches were SAR. Further, as is borne out from the statement of 'a Cabin employee Shri Rajendra Meena', the train halted at Godhra Railway Station until 7:48 am After the train started, there was a first chain pulling . In minutes the train again started and then there was second chain pulling at about 8:00 am Statement further reveals that the Fire Fighter reached at about 9:00-9:15 am Then the train was taken to the Yard and two coaches were separated. Again the train was brought to Platform No.10 and after the passengers re-boarded the train, it departed at about 12:45 am with the passengers.

I do not want to comment on the merits of the case which has stood judicial scrutiny. But the intent of the government through this entire compensation exercise was to give some sort of amnesty to those accused under POTA during the previous regime, whether it was the Godhra carnage or Ghatkopar, Mulund, Vile Parle, Bombay Central where the perpetrators were Saquib Nachan (ex SIMI leader) or Atif Nasir Mullah. Incidentally, I filed counter-affidavits in these cases also in the Bombay High Court in August 2009 and January 2010.

Further, during the High Court proceedings in the Godhra-Vaghela case in the Gujarat High Court on 1-2 February 2009, the Union of India engaged Additional Solicitor General Gopal Subramaniam, who convinced the court that the 'intent to commit a terror act' which was prerequisite for trial under POTA, could not be established. In this case, the government's Addl SG was arguing for a criminal, along with the criminal's lawyer, Nitya Ramakrishnan, one of the left-leaning advocates for whom rights of perpetrators are higher than rights of victims or citizens of this country and over and above national interests.

In a unique situation, the Government of Gujarat filed an SLP, No. 1444 of 2009, and the petitioner filed SLP No. 1700 of 2009. I recall these cases because during the course of discussion with Buch, I mentioned to him that an SLP between the State and the Centre is not good, the Special Leave Petition is basically a citizen's prerogative. For resolutions of differences between State and Centre, should we not take recourse to Article 130 of the Constitution?

The 17.7.2009 CMs' Conference

I had been more involved with the 17.7.2009 CMs' conference. Two new institutions were being carved out in the form of NATGRID and NCTC. It was basically about the Home Minister lecturing to the States about the new initiatives taken by the Ministry of Home Affairs and requesting the States to get involved and reap their benefits.

In addition, we had to take follow up action on the 26.11.2008 case, what with sharing of evidence with Pakistan. We also had to deal with institutional matters relating to the setting up of the NIA. Moreover, the MAC strengthening also required some rigorous work, requiring envisioning of structures, establishing them and locating funding for them.

The Ishrat Jahan case

At the time of writing, the Ishrat Jahan case was an ongoing criminal case in Gujarat, in which the relatives of the dead initially accused officers of the Ahmedabad Police Crime Branch and members of the Subsidiary Intelligence Bureau (SIB) of Ahmedabad of jointly having carried out a staged 'encounter killing' by shooting dead four people on 15 June 2004. Those killed in the incident were Ishrat Jahan Raza, a 19-year-old woman from Mumbra, Maharashtra, and three men – Javed Ghulam Sheikh (born Pranesh Pillai), Amjad Ali Rana and Zeeshan Johar.

Several officials associated with the case, including those from Home Ministry and Intelligence Bureau, later accused the then UPA government of changing a counter-affidavit (which I had filed) for political gains. The policemen accused of fake encounter have all denied the charges and appealed to higher courts for discharge. The Supreme Court has decided to hear the plea for quashing action against the Gujarat police.

In July 2009, we received a notice from the Gujarat High Court requiring MHA to file the 'factual position' in the case filed by Shamima Kauser, Ishrat Jahan's mother seeking compensation for custodial death of her daughter. She had, at the outset, called for investigation into the circumstances of her death alleging that it was a custodial death.

A similar notice was also received in respect of another case filed by Gopinathan Pillai, the father of Javed Mohammad Ghulam Shiekh alias Pranesh Kumar Pillai. This plea had been moved in the Supreme Court seeking compensation for the alleged custodial death of the son, which was remitted to the Gujarat High Court.

After perusing the notices, I had a meticulous junior locate the case papers quickly, we perused the inputs then available of this file and after obtaining further inputs from our agencies, I ventured to draft an affidavit (a counter-affidavit) in the case, making clear before the courts the Central government's (read the MHA's) position.

It then came to my notice that there had been an Affidavit (a counter) in the Ishrat Jahan case drafted and sent to the Assistant Solicitor General, Harin Raval at Ahmedabad in 2005. But it was never filed. Mine would be the second such MHA response. The '2005 counter-affidavit draft' is now reported to be missing from official records of the ASG's office.

After the second preliminary draft was made out, I sent the file to my Director (Internal Security) and he in turn sent it to the Joint Secretary (Internal Security), D Diptivilasa. The Joint Secretary directed me to do proper referencing, which we complied with. Thereafter, the file was sent to Home Minister Chidambaram via the Home Secretary.

The Minister approved it. That Chidambaram had appended his signature on it in approval has already been made public by several news channels through RTI in April 2016. Later it was also sent to the Law Secretary.

After the entire process of approval had been gone through, the fair affidavit was made out. I was then asked to file the government affidavit (counter-affidavit 2009) at Ahmedabad.

It was the day of Rakshabandhan which is also celebrated as Shraavan Pournami in my community. The day next to Shraavan Pournami, we propitiated goddess Gayatri in the morning. I distinctly recall having consulted my father, whether I could undertake the trip. He said 'yes' while suggesting that the special prayer to the goddess could be done in Ahmedabad early in the morning. He also gave me the *sankalpa* (resolve) for the occasion. Accordingly, I took an evening flight to Ahmedabad on 5.8.2009.

I generally stayed in a Central Police Force guest house in

the outskirts of Ahmedabad with a beautiful campus. The next morning I went to the office of the Assistant Solicitor General. His name was Pankaj S Champaneri. He asked me to wait in his chambers and left. After few rounds of *chai* and *farsan* (the Gujarati savouries which are very delicious) offered by his staff, I got restless. Champaneri returned on the stroke of 12. He told me that the affidavit could not be filed that day. Then I went to the High Registry. They told me that such affidavits could be filed up to 4:00 pm.

On my previous visits to the Gujarat High Court I had identified an eatery where the food was really delicious. It is just outside the High Court complex. I had a quick *thali* lunch there and came back to the office of the Assistant Solicitor General. I told him that I had spoken to the Registry and they had said, such affidavits could be filed up to 4:00 pm. Champaneri told me that he had spoken to the then Home Secretary, G K Pillai, who had instructed that the affidavit need not be filed. I called my Joint Secretary (IS), and Diptivilasa told me there was no such instruction. I went back to Champaneri and told him that I had spoken to JS (IS) and there was no such instruction. Champaneri then said that Additional Solicitor General Harin Raval had spoken to the Home Secretary. I called my office back to corroborate and confirm.

Thereafter, I went back and I confess, I tersely told Champaneri that I was a man from the MHA Secretariat and I took orders only from the Joint Secretary of the Division I was posted in. Hence, any orders had to be conveyed through him. After that there was a mild altercation. I was in discomfort because having been trained as a lawyer, I had many friends in this profession. I must confess that I was not happy about behaving in less than polite manner with this law officer. But this gentleman now started using dilatory tactics. Ultimately I told him, '...*mujhe apna order follow karna hai aur order hai ki affidavit file karo',* and started walking towards the Registry.

Fortunately, having been to this High Court on previous occasions in different cases, I was conversant with filing procedure as well as location of the places in the premises. Any newcomer would have lost his way around the Gujarat High Court premises trying to find where the Registry is located. It involved a very long walk through the corridors, right to the back of the building.

Even if one had located the Registry, there was a very elaborate procedure involved in filing counter-affidavits. There was a notice requirement to the concerned litigants which somehow got complied with through *dasti* (summons) to the respective lawyers whose munshis were fortunately present in the Registry premises. At that time, sensing the seriousness of the matter, the Assistant Solicitor General came running to the Registry, gasping for breath, accompanied by his munshi. This munshi, an affable old man known as Khan Sahib, ensured all requirements were fulfilled and got the counter-affidavit filed just before the closure time on 6 August 2009.

At that time, I did not know that this case would make history or that I will be a part of this history. I also did not know that this case would cause me so much trauma.

The MHA counter-affidavit, as ordered by the Gujarat High Court, had been filed. Hence, from the MHA side, the case had reached a level of finality. I, naturally, thought everything had been put to rest.

After the counter-affidavit

However, in September 2009 there were reports about an inquest being conducted on the exhumed bodies of the dead. A judicial officer called S P Tamang had conducted this inquest proceedings. Ishrat's mother had not requested this exhumation and the subsequent inquest. The magistrate's court had concluded that there was an encounter and there was no reason for such a killing. Therefore it was a 'fake' encounter. One thing the inquest could not establish is that any of the victims had carried weapons or themselves opened fire.

On 9 September 2009, the High Court of Gujarat Single Bench had stayed Tamang's report following Criminal Application No.13526 /2009 and Misc. Criminal Application No.10625 of 2009.

> Ld. Single Judge of the High Court vide the impugned Order dated 9.9.2009 stayed the Magisterial Enquiry Report (which had recorded that the encounter in which the petitioner's daughter was killed, was a fake) without recognizing that the said proceeding is statutory in nature, and thereby severely prejudiced the petitioner in her effort to obtain justice for her daughter.
>
> She could not participate in the Inquiry by Shri S.P. Tamang Metropolitan Magistrate as summon dated 13.8.2009, directing her to participate in the Inquiry was received only on 7.9.2009.

It was a case where the witness was zealous while the litigant was laid back. The entire process of reopening of the inquest by Judge Tamang was conducted on an application by some overzealous vested interest, whether political or nonpolitical, to further their own interest, keeping the next of kin in oblivion. Ishrat's mother or Pranesh's father had not known even of exhumation of their bodies and the subsequent inquest.

On learning of the inquest, I had called for the relevant papers and after having perused them, I had submitted my views, for orders on what to do.

In September 2009, the Home Minister was in the USA when this Tamang Report was being flashed on television and other media. He was accompanied amongst others by the Joint Secretary, Internal Security. The Home Minister of the State of

Gujarat displayed the MHA counter-affidavit signed and filed by me on 6.8.2009. The Joint Secretary later told us that after the media reports, his trip with the Minister was no longer comfortable. Upon his return to India, he called for the file. I must confess that was the last I saw of the file at that point in time. (The file, the media tells me, has gone missing.)

Thereafter, Home Minister Chidambaram, an eminent lawyer, with yet another eminent lawyer, set about to draft a supplementary affidavit to control the damage done by the MHA counter-affidavit.

I asked my seniors whether we can or if we have ever filed a supplementary affidavit? I was curtly asked to shut up and watch the game. I later learnt that this supplementary affidavit was not even called a 'supplementary'. It was given a new name by lawyer Chidambaram. It was called, 'further affidavit'. At the time of writing, this affidavit too is missing from records.[18]

After a few days, I was closeted with Director (IS) in his room in the evening. Evenings in the Room of Director (IS), which we called zero hour, were times when we would exchange, shout at each other, de-stress, convey our reservations/ constraints to him, argue with him and also find several solutions.

That evening we were having a very acrimonious altercation, The Under Secretary in charge of Parliamentary Work, Ajay Sumbly walked in with a paper which warranted the Director's

---

18 According to media reports, the papers, which disappeared from the Home Ministry, include the copy of an affidavit vetted by the then Attorney General and submitted in the Gujarat High Court in 2009 and the draft of the second affidavit vetted by the AG on which changes were made.

Two letters written by the then Home Secretary G K Pillai to the then Attorney General, late G E Vahanvati, and the copy of the draft affidavit have also so far remained untraceable. All the four IB officers accused of rights violations were handling the key Internal Security-I division in the Home Ministry as Joint Secretaries in different periods.

immediate attention. After perusing the document, our Director (IS) nonchalantly said, 'let's attend to this but our altercation is to be continued'. This serious fellow who had entered our room could not comprehend what was happening.

It was routine to assemble in the Director's room every evening. One evening, an envelope was received from the Home Minister's office, to be delivered to the Office/Home of the Attorney General of India. We deputed a dispatch rider from the Control Room to do this. After some time, the rider came back and informed us that the Attorney General was out of the country and would not be back before the 25th of the month.

I am not privy to any other incident after that except that I was given a draft of the supplementary (further) affidavit and asked to go and file it with the Ahmedabad court on behalf of the MHA on 28.9.2009.

As 29.9.2009 was Dussehra and the offices were closed, I booked myself on an evening flight to Ahmedabad on the 29th. I stayed at the same campus. The next morning, a personnel from the guard force was deputed to accompany me. Having stayed in this place, I knew many of the personnel posted there, so also this person. I had known the DIG in charge. I thought it was just a courtesy extended by the then DIG of the Centre.

Later on, when I was in the process of filing the supplementary (further affidavit) affidavit, I noticed this policeman/guard continuously giving an update on my movements and activities to someone on the mobile phone. I did not know, nor did I then ask to whom he was reporting. Much later, after several such instances during the trip, I solved the mystery. The office of the Home Minster had tracked my place of stay and through the headquarters of the Central Police Force, asked the station in charge to give an update on my movements. They wanted to ensure that the supplementary (further) affidavit was filed. I think they had little trust in me.

The reasons for this are, I had a good memory and remembered details and they always thought I knew too many things.

This had become a vice, not a virtue for the then Home Minister's establishment. I was identified as a man carrying too many things in my head, someone with a long memory. It is also believed that one of the main reasons for the 30.12.2008 incident was this and my chances would have been zero, had the kidnapping been successful.

On the balance, 2009 had been an eventful year for me in particular. Many friends and acquaintances had called me up saying they had read my name in the newspapers or seen me on television. But my father was a disturbed man. He said, the limelight was not good for me as I was identified now for the perpetrators and designers of terrorism. Now onward, I would always be at risk.

In retrospect, readers can deduce from the Sardarji Maghanji case, the Ishrat Jahan case and several such other cases that ever since the notification of the POTA Repeal Ordinance on 21.9.2004, the UPA government was more interested in bailing out those accused of terrorism than providing justice to victims. Was there any other interest working in the background?

The questions to ask would be, in how many cases has the Additional Solicitor General been engaged in defence of a person accused of crime? What was at stake in the Godhra-Vaghela case in February 2009? Was it not a terror case warranting trial under POTA which had stringent punishments and summary evidentiary process? Was the train burning not a crime under the IPC? Has any government ever engaged a law officer to protect the rights of an ordinary criminal vis-à-vis a victim of a crime or its survivors?

Eventful 2010: Charges counter-charges

THE DAWN OF 2010 came and we began to expect some calmness in the Internal Security front. We had taken control of the terrorism scene. Many sleeper cells had been neutralised through close cooperation and coordination between security agencies, law enforcing agencies with MHA, Internal Security Division acting as facilitator over the last three years.

The Agency Division which was generating inputs on many Pakistani/ PoK-based ISI sponsored cells, sleeper or active, was headed by Rajinder Kumar, a very committed IPS officer. We had never met as such except in one or two meetings in the OPS Room or some other senior officer's room. At that time, I did not even vaguely remember his face. He had to face a lot of harassment at the hands of the then government in power due to his pro-active stance against terrorism.

As fate would have it, in the case of Shamima Kauser, in which I filed the first MHA counter-affidavit, I was accused of having 'taken an affidavit' handed over by Rajinder Kumar, getting the approvals on this and had filed it in the Gujarat High Court on 6 August 2009. This illusion was perpetrated by the powers that be.

It is my personal conviction that there was an agenda behind this. This officer had caused the breaking up of and neutralisation of many sleeper cells through his visionary inputs. I always felt this outstanding officer had the capacity to sense the activities of these sleeper cells, no matter how low or insignificant these lay. I had over the period become a mobile information bank on counter-terror activities. Our diligence did not suit some people in the corridors of power who were partnering terror and colouring these with a shade identified with the majority religion. Hence, first they accused us of bias against minority communities and then associated our names in an unholy collaboration.

The 2010 CMs' Conference

In 2010, the third of the Chief Ministers' Conference was held on 7th February. I had, with the guidance of senior officers, especially Special Secretary (Internal Security) U K Bansal with whom I had spent several hours, developed a template covering 15 points for assessing the preparedness of State governments to react to terror attacks, disasters etc. These included QRT, coastal surveillance, disaster response mechanism, help lines, toll free lines, intelligence sharing etc.

During the conference, we felt that some of the State governments had also matured. Most Chief Ministers were handing out platitudes in their addresses, the 'secular' CMs mostly on saffron being the colour of terror. Just a few like Ashok Gehlot wanted to calibrate the new Home Ministry initiatives to the needs of their States.

There was a long lecture by the Lt Governor of Chandigarh, Shivraj Patil. He gave a long list of what steps can be taken to reinforce security, preparedness, preempt terror attacks and so on. A Tamil officer sitting next to me said, *'Gyanonodhayam'*, meaning dawn of knowledge and wisdom. I replied, *'Kan kurudu aanaduka apparam, Surya namaskaram'*, meaning, a blind man having lost sight is propitiating the Sun God (Lord of sight). Let him do it, today is Sunday.

Around the same time, Home Minister Chidambaram had made a reference to the existence of Saffron Terror in a speech in Darul-ul-Islam at Deoband in Saharanpur district of Uttar Pradesh.

However, then Chief Minister of Gujarat, Narendra Modi flagged a pertinent point. He told the gathering that transgression outside Indian territorial waters was a perennial problem for Gujarat's fisherman. This leads them to attendant problems. Hence, if they are engaged as territorial army soldiers, they would get trained in reading maps, compass and other such equipment. Also, being soldiers, they would be less vulnerable to poaching and compromise by Pakistani groups on the international sea route, which is quite rampant. Rather, they could be of help. Could the Ministry of Defence follow up on this?

The Chief Minister of Chhattisgarh, Raman Singh, also made a valuable suggestion regarding the selection criteria for recruitment to the Indian Reserve Battalion. The health standards, including height prescribed for it, is standardised across the States. He suggested, this should be made State specific. In his State, there were certain communities which were hardy, though traditionally of short height and they do not get selected. Hence there are incidences of disaffection.

During the lunch break, some senior officers of the Director General of Police, some Joint Secretaries etc. had come out for a smoke break. Since it was time for resumption of the session, I had gone over to request them to rejoin the session. This also included a Director General of a paramilitary force, Raman

Srivastava, who had not long before been our Special Secretary (IS), with whom I enjoyed a level of comfort and familiarity. They were discussing another officer in the Ministry of Home Affairs, in the Police Modernisation Division, who was unnecessarily delaying procurement decisions. There was a general feeling of consensus that this delay was actually crippling the real-time functioning of the paramilitary forces and the Home Secretary had asked the man, Dharmendra Sharma, to proceed on leave, although he had the support of the Home Minister.

After lunch I was called by M A Siddique, Private Secretary to the Home Minister, and asked to locate an officer who was then Special Director, CBI. Sharad Chandra Sinha was to report to the Home Minister immediately. Accordingly, after scouting the Vigyan Bhavan main conference hall and consulting a few colleagues to confirm that it was the same person, I found Sinha in the middle rows in the centre half of the hall. I conveyed the ministry's summons, asking him to meet the Home Minister in the ante room where other dignitaries like the PM, NSA M K Narayanan, Principal Secretary to PM, T K A Nair were also present.

I am given to understand that it was at the CM's conference ante-room that Sinha was told he would be the next DG NIA. We do not know what ACC procedure was followed and whether it was followed at all. It may be recalled that in those days, when a matter of avenging the loss of life of any security force officer was to be decided, the concerned Cabinet Committee members wanted 14 to 15 days' time to frame their position. But to appoint a person of their own choice on a nomination basis, without a choice of three names etc.—that could be decided over a lunch in a conference. Notwithstanding, two main members of the ACC were there and it was their call and they were exercising their powers.

German Bakery blast

Thereafter, on 8th February we had a very serious input. I placed it before the Director (IS). He personally drafted an advisory communication to three States which had Chabad Houses (place of worship and seminary for Jewish worshippers). The advisory communication was signed by the concerned Joint Secretary and issued. There was imminent threat of fidayeen attacks to these places and their vicinity. According to information available with the Home Ministry, Chabad Houses were located in Mumbai, Pune, Bangalore and Kochi. Hence the States of Maharashtra, Karnataka and Kerala were sensitised on 8 February 2010.

The input shared by the Home Ministry proved right. On 13 February 2010, there was a bomb blast in a German Bakery very close to the Chabad House in Pune. As many as 67 people died and many were injured.

This was a blast which could have been avoided. It appears that the Central alert was not taken seriously by the State government and even the Commissioner of Police, Pune, did not receive the input from the government of Maharashtra.

Or was it a deliberate policy not to share the input?

I ask this question because of certain information on funds used for terror attack. It is a stated fact that finance is the lifeline of terrorism. MHA had received the input on the funds used for the German Bakery attack. It was traced to Moshin Akbar Chowdhury and many such Akbar Chowdhurys. As many as eight accounts in the Ratnakar Bank, Pune with last names as Akbar Chowdhury were frozen under Section 51 A of UAPA Act.

This amendment was introduced in the new initiatives of the new Home Minister. But it was basically to meet the FATF membership criteria. Hence, these Bills were introduced under Article 253 of Indian Constitution, ie. a bill introduced to meet international commitments.

At that time, it came to light that the real Akbar Chowdhury was a poor man. All these eight Akbar Chowdhurys were only dummy account holders (*benami*). There were some political entities belonging to the then ruling coalition who controlled them. One such entity was a big hawala dealer, a man known as Baba Siddiqui from Mumbai with political links.

After the German Bakery blast, the Home Minister undertook a trip to Pune. Even his departure was delayed because Suresh Kalmadi, the then Member of Parliament from Pune, wanted to accompany the Minister. Kalmadi, now accused in the Commonwealth Games (CWG) scam, delayed the departure of the MHA team led by Chidambaram by few hours, perhaps giving enough time to vested interests, to engineer and manipulate evidences under the garb of crime scene protection.

Another head rolls

Immediately after the German Bakery Blast, the Budget Session of Parliament commenced. As usual, MHA was receiving literally hundreds of notices for questions and other motions. One such question was regarding the 'onward passage of evidence collected in the Mumbai blasts', sharing this with Pakistan. Only three persons, including the Joint Secretary (IS), were privy to the exact information, so the reply was drafted at that level.

This happened on 1 March 2010. It was the day of Holi which was a holiday. The Joint Secretary framed the reply that, 'intercepts furnished by State Investigation Agency have been examined and were shared with Pakistani authorities'.

Minister Chidambaram who had knocked off some intercepts from the basket to be shared with Pakistan, had amended the MHA answer for Parliament to read as, 'All intercepts received have been shared'. This was, of course, not the full truth.

No officer ever dares to lie in a Parliament question. Firstly, out of conscience and professionalism and secondly due to possible attendant consequences. The Joint Secretary (IS) re-submitted the file, reiterating his draft. Again the Union Minister modified it, holding his position which was less than the full truth. We were all oblivious of these happenings at the time. Subsequently, on the next working day, it appears the Minister ceded but made an unwanted remark on the file. The file never came back to the desk-level but the reply approved by the then Home Minister was placed in the table of the House. The reply to Lok Sabha Starred question no 78 answered on 2.3.2010 was, 'intercepts have been shared' and not all intercepts have been shared.

Later in the day, there was a meeting in the Home Secretary's chamber. My Director asked me to go to then Home Secretary's chamber and said he would go and fetch the Joint Secretary. But when we were settling down to the meeting in the HS's chamber, Director (IS) came sans Joint Secretary Diptivilasa and whispered in my ears that, *JS ka transfer ho gaya* (the JS has been transferred). The Home Secretary also confirmed the news at the outset of the meeting.

It would be best that a comparison of the inventory of intercepts used in the Ajmal Kasab trial and that shared with the Pakistani authorities be made in order to understand what difference the intercept evidence can make to such bilateral processes. I am fully aware that immediately, Pakistan will try to create a fuss and try to use such evidence as an alibi. But the nation should know. Posterity should know, how and where MHA stood in such matters in 2010. It was not the institution, the Ministry that called the shots, it was the Minister, the individual who did.

More importantly, the incumbent who replaced the persistent Joint Secretary was Dharmendra Sharma, the one who had been asked to proceed on leave by the Home Secretary in February for delaying procurement and adversely affecting the efficiency of the Central paramilitary forces. Was this again by design? We do not know.

Madhuri Gupta and friends

The only thing that came to light in 2010 was that there were a few CBI raids in the MHA on account of the Prevention of Corruption Act. This was very unusual. Inducement-related corruption was never heard of in MHA. There might have been cases of nepotism, recommendations for postings, the usual *jugaad*, the gift seeking like whiskeys or requests for vehicles with Central paramilitary forces. These specific incidents were never actually reported. These were all hearsay. But two cases came to light in 2010.

According to a CBI statement in April, a senior Indian Railway Service Officer attached to the Ministry of Home Affairs, Radhey Shyam Sharma was accused of taking a bribe of Rs 10 lakh. This Sharma, in charge of procurements, was also accused of procuring bulletproof jackets illegally.

The charges against R S Sharma were brought immediately after Madhuri Gupta, incumbent Second Secretary in the High Commission of India, Islamabad was summoned to Delhi in April 2010 and arrested from the Delhi Airport. She was charged with leaking classified information to Pakistan's ISI.

Was it a mere coincidence? It may appear to be so to the naked eye. Sharma was handling procurements for Central paramilitary forces and the deployment in different sensitive locations can be given away by consignee location of the order. Gupta was leaking sensitive information. What more sensitive information is valuable to Pakistan ISI than locations of Indian paramilitary forces, their relative strengths in terms of equipment, instruments, and other inventory?

Obviously it was an intelligence-driven operation and the country should be grateful to our agencies. One of the officers of the busting team, IB Special Director Rajinder Kumar, was accused of Human Rights violations in the Ishrat Jahan Case and his retirement benefits were denied. Not the best way to decorate an illustrious officer.

Television clips of December 2010 will tell my readers that in December 2010, another MHA official, Pradeep Singh, dealing with giving critical security clearances to foreign investments, working in the MHA's Foreigners Division, was accused by the CBI of corruption. At the same time, Dr Ravinder Singh, who as Director IS had been handling many a sensitive document and subjects (including the Blackberry dispute in which Home Ministry had asked the Canadian company RIM, the maker of Blackberry phone, to give the government access to their secret codes for security reasons) was also raided. Both these officials had been under the supervision of Joint Secretary Dharmendra Sharma in Police Modernization Division and who had oversight of the procurement work.

Were the security clearances being issued without due diligence? Was the security of several establishments and infrastructure projects being built by private players being compromised? Were the proposals considered for Foreign Investments in sectors in which security clearances are used as vital input by the Board being diluted? Or were people like Rajinder Kumar, Pradeep Singh and Ravinder Singh the scapegoats while the big fish played free? We do not know.

Surgical Strikes

While discussing security of vital installations, I would also like to bring out a very interesting fact. In September 2016, there were surgical strikes which were a calibrated initiative to arrest the misdeeds of Pakistan and other ISI-sponsored groups operating from PoK. In the aftermath of these surgical strikes, there were statements issued by several political entities about how there were surgical strikes even during 2006-2010 etc.

Before every such strike is planned, there is a group of top officials of security establishments who assess the possible fallouts of such strikes. Then there are prescribed procedure stipulated for securing the most important assets of the nation. These are contained in the form of a manual. This contains several calibrations commensurate with the index and degree of offensive proposed. The order comes from the top security establishment. There is clear demarcation of responsibility between the two leading Ministries, Home and Defence. These top security orders are put in place before commencement of the process of any 'surgical strikes'. I never received any orders to implement any of the safeguards during 2006-2010 in the MHA.

Was the government of the day being reckless in not invoking this procedure before initiating the surgical strikes, in case they did carry out such a strike as claimed? Was the government of the day throwing caution to winds? Were they not exposing our assets? This is on the assumption that the claim of surgical strikes is true. Or else, the claim is untrue.

Exiled from Internal Security

Joint Secretary Diptivilasa, leader of a very cohesive group, had been replaced. The new incumbent, Dharmendra Sharma, was an erudite person. He had this tendency to keep polishing the drafts. It was expected to be in the best of English language, no matter how inordinately delayed the document got. One day, I had the temerity to remark, *'Sirji, angrezi polish hote hote, terrorist goli maar jayega'*. He did not take kindly to this smart crack. Anyways, a controversy surrounding me was brewing.

The administration Division of MHA manages the deployment of resources—human resources, facilities, utilities, supply of consumables etc. I had space constraints. I needed separate steel almirahs for ensuring the safe custody of Fake Currency Notes seized by our security forces. I had requested for the same. The practice was, I used to go to Mumbai to hand them over to the Reserve Bank of India for getting them to do the examination. Till that time, the notes were my responsibility.

I had asked the Administration Division for providing me an almirah. They had a Director who had this habit of crying shortage of resources. He was also close to the Additional Secretary (BM), who had caused the extension of stay of the Indian delegation in Pakistan during 26/11. Since operational requirement was on the agenda in one meeting, the Home Secretary desired to know whether I had any constraints, I conveyed my requirement to him. This set off a level of hostility from these Administration personnel.

Outside my chamber, apart from my staff, the Police Training Section was also occupying space. There was a lady officer in charge. One fine morning, I was asked to give my handwriting specimen for examination before the Joint Secretary (Administration). Later I came to know that the lady officer occupying the space outside my room had made a gender harassment complaint against me. The allegations were that a nasty, handwritten note was found along with a packet of condoms in her table drawer. After that an inquiry was initiated as per the Vishaka guidelines and nothing was found. It was obviously a frame-up. I do not know if it was due to personal malice or it was a larger design.

I was transferred from the IS Division in June 2010.

It is a matter of public record that the existence of Hindu Terrorism was first recorded by Joint Secretary Dharmendra Sharma in a file, without attendant and corresponding inputs from any agency for the first time in July 2010. Hence my transfer from the IS Division in June appears to be a design to me.

The Kashmir problem

Later, I was posted in the Kashmir Division of the MHA. Here my tenure was very short. So I do not vividly remember details. The only achievement was that when a group of eminent citizens led by the illustrious journalist Dilip Padgaonkar and Radha Kumar, an academician and others, decided to try for peace in Kashmir, I wrote a paper—relying upon 1953, 1975, 1984 and other series of agreements—that Kashmir had no problem that requires resolution.

'Kashmir trouble' is basically a commercial venture. When the Prime Minister's Rs 5,500 crore package of 2006, or a subsequent Rs 26,000 crore package (which ultimately benefits the contractors and separatist) has been expended, new ventures like stone-pelting start. I had forecast this June 2010 disturbance in the last week of May itself.

In fact, in May 2010, many of my ex-colleagues were surprised that I could forecast a disturbance with very little exposure to Kashmir affairs.

Vilfredo Pareto, an Italian Sociologist, had propounded a theory. According to him, the governing elites come to political power due to existence of some malfunction in society and with a promise of solution to this malfunction. However, after coming to power, they ensure that this malfunction continues and perpetrates so that their continuation in power on this pretext is ensured.

The issue of Kashmir and its illusory problem, and non-resolution of the problem if it exists, and non-removing the veil of illusion if it doesn't exist, is an apt validation of this theory.

My paper set the cat amongst the pigeons.

As expected, it was trashed and destroyed. Thereafter, I felt unwanted in MHA. There was this fear also that I could be framed any time after one gender harassment case, which a staffer from Administration known to me from Udyog Bhavan days, leaked. He said that it was a frame-up. After that I decided to leave Delhi for a while. I took up a new posting in Mumbai in the Central Board of Film Certification.

However, I was kept up to date about the happenings in the MHA through my former colleagues. I learnt that after the departure of Joint Secretary Diptivilasa and myself from the IS Division, the Director also proceeded on long leave on the pretext that his children had examinations. Thus, for those who wanted us out, effectively, the Internal Security Division's best team had been neutralised. Of course, the other Director, Dr Singh who was in the Division, had already attained notoriety in the software/hardware case.

Their victories

After suspension of Home Secretary Level Talks in the aftermath of 26.11.2008, the next edition of talks was hosted by India in New Delhi at the end of March 2011. I have no information on what led to this resumption of talks. The very fact that the HSLTs were resumed meant, the opposite party (or collaborative party) emerged the winner.

It is important to mention that during these talks, dossiers were exchanged between the delegations on fugitives. In 2006, 2007 and 2008, MHA IS Division was assigned the task of coordinating the dossier preparation. We used to interact closely with agencies, do cross verification and then one of the agencies was tasked with the final printing of the dossier. The Home Secretary himself chaired the meetings in the iteration process. Hence the information contained in the dossier was accurate to the sigma level. We knew there was zero margin of error.

But the new team had assigned the work to their new agency, that is the NIA, which was the then Home Minister's favourite. I do not know what was the level of quality control. I do not know whether they really coordinated with other agencies. They took their orders from P Chidambaram. During the initial stages, the personnel of the Agency were well aware of this. They behaved vis-à-vis the other agencies as if they were one notch above. Hence, it appears they did not take the other agencies on board. This was a recipe for disaster. It happened.

Two of the names included in the Indian dossier given to the Pakistan visitors in 2011 were that of Wazhul Kamar Khan and one more. These two were indicated as 'fugitives from Indian law living in Pakistan'. They were found lodged in Indian jails! NIA perhaps should have been more diligent. Or were they under orders to commit this error? We do not know. But the end result was that credibility of all the dossiers which India had painstakingly prepared with the agencies crashed. Pakistan went home laughing. The Home Minister found two sub-inspectors responsible and suspended them. Later, he admitted to the media his own responsibility.

> A day after it emerged that one of the 50 fugitives named in the list given by India to Pakistan in March was living in Thane, Union Home Minister P Chidambaram took 'responsibility' for the 'mistake'.
>
> Wazhul Kamar Khan alias Murtuza Choudhary, who was arrested last year for his alleged role in the 2003 Mulund blasts, got on to the list as a result of a 'genuine error' by Mumbai Police and 'oversight' by the Intelligence Bureau, Chidambaram told reporters today.
>
> The list of fugitives from Indian law hiding out in Pakistan was part of the dossier handed over by Union Home Secretary G K Pillai to his counterpart Qamar Zaman Choudhary on March 28, 2011.
>
> Chidambaram said that Mumbai Police arrested Khan on May 21, 2010, but did not inform CBI or request the withdrawal of the Red Corner Notice (RCN) against him. CBI made inquiries with Mumbai Police about Khan on January 27 this year, he said, adding that Mumbai Police wrote to the government yesterday, requesting cancellation of the RCN.

'We take responsibility. It is a mistake. How this mistake has happened has been explained subsequently. CBI through Interpol will notify the arrest of Khan', Chidambaram said. He also said that Khan's name had already been removed from the list of wanted, and asserted that what had happened was not a 'monumental mistake' of 'calamitous consequence'. The minister revealed that Mumbai Police had in January this year conveyed to the Intelligence Bureau (IB) office in Mumbai that Khan had been arrested.

'This information, unfortunately, was not reflected in the list of fugitives maintained by the authorities and was overlooked while a list was prepared in March 2011', he said. It was clear that the failure on the part of Mumbai Police to formally communicate the fact of the arrest of Khan to the CBI had resulted in the name being retained by CBI, Chidambaram said. 'It is possible that the said failure was the result of a genuine oversight by the Mumbai Police. At the same time there was also a lapse on the part of IB in not reflecting the information received by it while preparing the list in March 2011.'

(Source *Express News Service* May 2011)

In one stroke the credibility of all the dossiers painstakingly prepared by India, year after year, for different bilateral mechanisms had been destroyed.

It is not the credibility of our documents before international media and agencies alone. Chidambaram had also betrayed the falsity of his responses that had been tabled in both Houses of Parliament to question after question on the steps taken to combat terror. Statements like these sounded so hollow:

Our security concerns are conveyed in various bilateral mechanisms established for this purpose.

The government pursues a multi-dimensional approach to deal with terrorists activities and extends supports to the States in neutralizing such terrorist activities.

The Government has taken measures which include strengthening of border management to check infiltration, galvanizing the intelligence machinery, ensuring improved technology, weaponry and equipment, of security forces both at the Centre and the States, by well coordinated intelligence based operations. Besides, steps have also been taken to achieve bilateral and multilateral cooperation to deal with the menace of terrorism, given its global dimensions.

Life after MHA

MY TENURE IN the Central Board of Film Certification was generally routine and uneventful. I had to attend meetings in the Ministry of I&B almost every weekend. The area of operation was new and interesting. The organisation had lots of problems with lack of staff, unmotivated human resources, corruption and with nine field offices for oversight. Soon after my joining, another Chief Executive Officer also took over. We set about cleaning of the organisation. This Chief Executive Officer was a lady Customs and Excise Service officer. There was a general level of cordiality between us. She was very polite and empathetic in her dispensation with staff. I do believe that while dealing with sub-optimally productive staff, one has to wield the stick. *Motivation gaya tel lene*. But this lady was too accommodative.

In the Ministry there was Joint Secretary D P Reddy, who expected too much. His common refrain was: *arre tum home ministry mein itna kuch kiya, yahan kya problem hai*? He acted tough with me. But I always knew, underneath he was a lovely officer. I continued for nearly one-and-a-half years in the I&B Ministry. To mitigate corruption, I worked with NIC personnel and introduced online application for film certification which was inaugurated by the Chief Minister of Maharashtra and the then Chairperson CBFC, Leela Samson, the dancer in Mumbai in June 2011. I knew within a year, I had made a mark. But I could never settle down to life in Mumbai. My wife was still in Delhi. My son had completed his Engineering course and had joined MBA in Delhi. So I longed to be in Delhi. Initially, I politely requested for a change. It was curtly turned down. After a few tantrums and the threat of VRS, I was finally returned to Delhi.

It was December 2011. I was placed in the Ministry of Urban Development, in the Urban Transport Division. This Division also dealt with the finalisation of specification for buses procured under the JNNURM. In the meanwhile, my son who was a mechanical engineer, started working on projects with major bus manufacturers. I wanted to avoid conflict of interest. I informed my office, who promptly posted me as a Deputy Land and Development Officer.

I knew it was a challenging posting. Initially, I was given 'enforcement', a department which does the job of mapping encroachment on government lands and gets them cleared. At the outset, there was no proper record of encroachments. I got them all computerised and introduced a database. Surprisingly, the data mapped by this department is up to 9 July 2012 when I was assigned other responsibilities.

In July 2012 there was a Presidential election. The sitting Finance Minister, Pranab Mukherjee, had become the President of India. Hence there was general inquisitiveness as to who would be the next Finance Minister. Surprisingly, that very day, the then government appointed the sitting Home Minister, P Chidambaram, as the Finance Minister.

On the same day, as a result of grid failure, north India was plunged into darkness and 700 million people are said to have been without electricity that night. The incident was attributed to some failure on the management of the then Ministry of Power. The Power Minister was Sushil Kumar Shinde. Shinde, the Power Minister who had plunged the entire north India into darkness, was rewarded. Believe it or not, he became the new Home Minister! Metaphorically, he was to bring the same darkness in managing the security of the country.

Every day many Indians pray, *Tamaso Ma Jyotirgamaya*, meaning lead me from darkness to light. But we had a government which was doing the converse. The security of the people of the country was being entrusted to a person on the biggest day of his failure in the Power Ministry. We had a non-decisive Defence Minister in A K Antony and again we were given an indifferent Home Minister. Many from the security establishments could see the design in this. If people were secure, it was by the grace of God.

I was to oversee the projects of the National Building Construction Corporation. One of its ongoing projects at the time was the New Moti Bagh General Pool Residential Accommodation project, a green site which had to be brought to a closure. This project was being monitored by Secretary (Urban Development). He was a resident of the residential colony and hence had first-hand information of the shortcomings. There were many challenges of maintenance, water billings, stray dogs etc. Also one religious structure had come up behind the Leela Hotel which had bought the land in New Moti Bagh GPRA area on auction. The sale of land to the hotel enabled financing of the project. I got the orders and as per established and proper procedure, had the religious structure demolished in its embryonic stage.

This prompted an officer of the DDA to contact me for

guidance. He was under pressure from certain groups who were claiming a religious structure as an 'ancient and historical' one. There was lot of political pressure. I suggested to him to locate the satellite images of the year 2008-2009 etc. and place it on record. The papers were put up to Tejendra Khanna, LG, who was the Chairman of DDA. The LG upheld the decision that it was a new religious structure and then it was demolished. It is a different matter that on that very day, the LG was replaced by the Vice-Chancellor of Jamia Millia Islamia University, Najeeb Jung.

I also expedited the land use rights for the DMRC Phase III project. Actual process of allotment involved elaborate procedures and would have taken a long time. I helped them get the right of early entry and usage, so that the project could meet deadlines. Soon, I acquired the image of a very positive and result-oriented officer.

Back to the Ishrat Jahan case

However, the wheels of my fortune changed.

On 21.6.2013, I received a call from a Special Investigation Team of the CBI, Ahmedabad, asking me to appear before them on 22.6.2013 to record my statement.[19] It was the team which was investigating the Ishrat Jahan case. I curtly told them that they better send their formal request to Secretary

19 After the killings, an investigation was launched based on allegations that the description of the incident by the police was false and the killings were deliberate and unlawful. The police team involved in the incident had been led by DIG DG Vanjara, an officer who spent eight years in jail for his alleged involvement in the extrajudicial killing of another person, Sohrabuddin Sheikh. Five years later, in 2009, an Ahmedabad Metropolitan court ruled that the encounter was staged. The decision was challenged by the State and taken to the Gujarat High Court. After further investigation, in 2011, a Special Investigation Team (SIT) told the High Court that the encounter was not genuine, and the victims were killed prior to the date of the staged encounter.

CENTRAL BUREAU OF INVESTIGATION
SPECIAL INVESTIGATION TEAM (ISHRAT JAHAN CASE)
2ND FLOOR, PATNAGAR YOJNA BHAVAN, BLOCK A,
SECTOR 16, GANDHINAGAR (GUJARAT)
PHONE : 079-23241682, 23241683, TELEFAX : 079-23241681

No. RC/5/S/2011/Mum/SIT (Ishrat)/Inv/ 529/2013 — **Date: 21.06.2013**

To

Dr. Sudhir Krishna, IAS
Secretary,
Ministry of Urban Development,
Nirwan Bhavan, New Delhi. (011-23061459)

Office of Secy. (UD)
Dy. No. 3661-D
Date 21/6/13

Subject: **Investigation of RC-5(S)/2011 of CBI, SCB, Mumbai relating to the encounter death of Ms. Raza Ishrat Jahan and 3 others – reg.**

Sir,

On the orders of Hon'ble High Court of Gujarat vide order dated 01.12.2011, the case in Crime No. DCB PS 1 CR No. 8/2004 relating to the encounter death of Ms. Raza Ishrat Jahan and 3 others was handed over to CBI, SCB, Mumbai and being investigated by the undersigned.

In connection with the investigation of the above mentioned case, Shri R V S Mani, the then Under Secretary (Home), Internal Security- VI, MHA, New Delhi presently working as Dy. Land & Development Officer, New Delhi may kindly be deputed to attend CBI, SIT, Gandhinagar, Gujarat on 22.06.2013 at 10:00 hrs for his examination with regard to the said case.

High Court related matter (Most Urgent)

Yours faithfully,
21/06/2013.
(G.Kalaimani)
Dy. SP/Chief Investigating Officer,
CBI-SIT (Ishrat Jahan case)
Camp : Gandhinagar

ISHRAT JAHAN CASE * CBI SIT *

Government of India
Ministry of Urban Development
Land and Development Office

I received a telephonic summon from Special Investigation Team of CBI (SIT), that I should be present in Gandhi Nagar, Gujarat on 22.06.2013 regarding recording of my statement in the Ishrat Jehan case. I suggested that they should convey the said summon in written through Secretary of Ministry of Urban Development who in effect is the owner of my services at present. Accordingly, a letter was received late in the evening which is placed below which inter alia also explains the background of the summons.

2. Accordingly, I proceeded to Gandhi Nagar after due approval of the travel schedule by the competent authority I went to Gandhi Nagar on 22.6.2013. During the course of recording of the statement, there were differences between the facts in my knowledge and the framing of the same by the IG, SIT, Shri Satish Chandra Verma. Many a fact to which I was not privy to or officially never in my domain during the tenure in Ministry of Home Affairs were coerced to be signed by me. Knowing fully well that this would tantamount falsely indicting of my seniors at the extant time, I declined to sign any statement. They have recorded some contents under the premise the Section 161 of Cr. P. C. does not require signature of the witness.

3. In view of the above it is my request that, in future I shall be willing to record the statements to CBI only in the presence of CVO or his authorized representative of the Ministry as well as after the contents have been duly vetted by Ministry of Home Affairs.

4. This may kindly be taken up with the Ministry of Home Affairs so that appropriate arrangements could be worked out.

5. I may also be permitted to engage the services of a lawyer to be present while recording my statement, because many contents are sought to be included and I am being coerced to sign the statement by the CBI.

6. Due to paucity of time, this case could not be processed as per laid down procedure. However, since this is matter involving CBI, it may be appropriately processed in the file of Vigilance Section of Ministry of Urban Development, which is the CVO's Secretariat.

(R.V.S. Mani)
Dy.L&DO(V)
24.6.2013

L&DO (On leave)

JS(LW)

The following have been conveyed by me to IG.SIT

(Recalled from Memory)

Brief facts about my joining Government Service and career path etc including date of joining MHA (All matters of record).

About my responsibilities as US (IS VI) which inter alia including supervising the work of IS-VI Section dealing with Counter Terrorism, Combating FICN, servicing Special Economic Intelligence Cell, Core Group on Growth of Religious Institutions in both Indo Bangladesh and Indo Nepal Borders.

This case related to IS IV Section. It was explained to him that I also used to supervise the work of IS IV Section in consultation with Director (IS-II) from time to time. IS IV deals with Law and Order and Intelligence Coordination.

I also made it clear that I had as and when Director (IS-II) or JS(IS-I) requested me I had dealt with work of other sections especially those relating to litigation matters. I had dealt with Sardaji Maganji Vaghela (Abdul Sheikh Kalota Case) in Gujarat High Court, Jagjit Singh Hawara Case in Punjab and Haryana High Court etc which related to IS VII Section. I had attended meetings in the Department of IT/ FIPB Meetings as a stand by which related to IS-II Section. Hence, we used to function as a team. There have been instances where my colleague have attended to my work like notification of UAPA Act/ NIA Act on 31.12.2008 etc. It was emphasized to him that we used to work as a team.

The working methodology of IS-I Division, as to how we proceed to get inputs from IB, R&AW and other intelligence agencies and take orders and appropriately sensitized the State Governments.

He asked me how the Counter Affidavit was drafted. It was explained to him that generally myself and Director (IS-I) used to draft affidavits together. I did not specifically remember, but it must have been drafted in the same manner.

He asked me whether this affidavit filed on 6.6.2009, was brought as a draft by Rajinder Kumar which was then submitted for approval. I said it is not the case. He asked me who brought this Affidavit. I said Director (IS-II) being an Income Tax Officer as well as my being a qualified lawyer do not required any other person to draft it for us.

He asked why I am trying to collude with Mr. Rajinder Kumar. I said that is not the case. He said you know Mr. Rajinder Kumar well. I said I have seen in one or two meetings relating Pakistan. He was member of Indian delegation during Home Secretary Level Talks with Pakistan, in 2006. I had arrange the delegation to use then VIP lounge and it is the first time I saw Mr. Rajinder Kumar. Thereafter, he was a member if Indian delegation during the HSLT-2007, held in Le Meridien Hotel Delhi when I saw him for the second time. Other than during meeting on any Pakistan related issues I was not required to meet Mr. Rajinder Kumar.

He asked me whom I used to interact with in IB. I said I interacted only with Mr. D.P. Sinha on Law and Order or his deputy one Mr. Deka, Mr. Ashok Prasad his deputies Mr. Harmeet Sing (upto 2007), Mr. Prabhaka Alok and Mr. H.K. Mishra, Deputy Directors and Mr. Santosh Chandran and Col. Isenhower, Asst. Directors. ON financing issues the interaction was with Mr. Udyan Mukherjee for a short period, then only Mr. Ritwik Rudra was the Deputy Director. Further on the issues of Sikh Jatha to Pakistan, Mr. Ritwkik Rudra and one Mr. Meena Assistant Director were the officials.

He stated that I say you are lying. You were interacting with Rajinder Kumar. Your seniors Mr. P.K. Mishra, Director and Mr. Diptivilasa, Joint Secretary were interacting with Mr. Rajinder Kumar. I told him that I reiterate my position which can be confirmed from records. As records my seniors it was none of by business nor yours as to whom they used to meet for official work.

He stated that all the Home Ministry is stooge of the IB. I told him that we are not fools sitting here in MHA Secretariat. Every IB input is processed and only then action is taken.

He said in this case it is not an input. If Javed Ghulam Sheikh had two passports or they purchased arms from Ibrahimpur or traveled to Lucknow it is not intelligence input but based on investigation after killing them

I said it is your perception. For me personally this is an intelligence input. You do not have to kill a person to collect information on this. Two passports can be traced through records even when the man is alive. Information on purchase of arms from wherever it is can be collated and that is what is the job of IB. If you can prove otherwise, you are free to do so.

He said why do rely on IB's input ? I told him that there is no reason not to rely on the same. Further, there have been many modules busted relying upon the input. He asked me specific numbers. I told this information will be available in IS.I Section of MHA. For specific periods we have quoted these numbers year wise in many Parliament Questions answered during the period. This is in public domain.

Further, I told him as per my knowledge many terrorists attacks have been averted based on close coordination between intelligence agencies and state security agencies. This position has been conveyed in Allahabad High Court on 5.1.2008, Supreme Court/ Kolkata High Court etc. Further this position has also been conveyed in reply to many Parliament Questions.

He asked me whether the Government Counsel (Mr. PS Champaneri, Ld. ASG as informed by me) raised any objection to filing the Affidavit. I conveyed that he had objected and I conveyed the position to JS(IS.I)/ Director (IS.II) and as a sequel he received instructions to file and so the Affidavit was filed.

He repeated all of you are stooges of IB. He told that to become Home Secretary one has to have IB Clearance. There is no Parliamentary oversight on IB. IN the instant case. Gujarat High Court on 24.8.2010 ordered an IPS officer to be nominated to SIT. Your Mr. Diptivilasa transfers himself to

JS(IPS) and nominates IB stooge, Mr. Karnal Singh who was JCP (Special Cell), Delhi Police which is an extension of IB. He narrated that he fought with him and so Mr. Karnal Singh left.

I told him I had left the Ministry. But Mr. Diptvilase's transfer took place in March 2010 to IS-II Division. From there when he was transferred to IPS Division is not in my knowledge.

He told me you are chamcha of Mr. Diptivilasa otherwise how come both are in the same Ministry. It told him to desist from making such baseless comments. As regards my posting in Ministry of Urban Development, he may ask his own Administrative Ministry, if he trusts them, i.e. Department of Personnel and Training.

He started narrating as to how the 13.12.2001 attack on Parliament of India and 26.11.2008 attacks are orchestrated by the Government in power. He stated that both these were with the objective of strengthening the counter terrorist legislation. He narrated that 13.12.2001 was followed by POTA and 26.11.2008 was followed by amendment to UAPA wherein even and Rupees 10 in any body's pocket can be treated for proceeds of terrorism.

I told him that he is entitled to his view but such view is generally held as ISI's view in the security establishment.

At the end Mr. Verma dictated a note indicating that two IB persons came to the room of Director (IS-II) with a Draft Affidavit which was put up for approval and after approval filed on 6.6.2009. Thereafter, since the said Affidavit was misinterpreted by the Government of Gujarat, on orders from Home Minister, another Affidavit was drafted in the Room of JS(IS.I) with representatives from Ministry of Law, IB etc and the same was filed on 29.9.2009.

I refused to sign the statement and he directed the DSP to treat use it as Statement under Section 161 of Cr. P.C. I told him that anything other than fact, I will retract it under Section 164 of Cr.P.C.

(Urban Development). Accordingly, they sent a formal request to the Secretary's office. The Secretary was on an official visit to London. The Staff Officer to the Secretary spoke to him over telephone and obtained his orders, and told the Joint Secretary that I could respond to the CBI request. Accordingly I got a ticket to Ahmedabad by early morning flight on 22.6.2013. What transpired at Gandhi Nagar between myself and my able friend Satish Verma, IPS who posed as the Inspector General of SIT, is all over the media and is now a matter of public record.

Why do I say Satish Verma 'posed' as the IG of SIT?

He has not denied this in spite of it being in the public domain. But later, at leisure, when I was trying to locate the authority of the SIT, I chanced upon the Gujarat High Court Order of 1.12.2011. There had been several orders prior to this, constituting and revising the SIT. But I could not access any High Court Order after this date on the subject. The order of the

Gujarat High Court was very clear and specific. Satish Verma, a police officer who was a part of the first SIT, had a clear role. He was *not* to conduct any investigation. The fresh investigation for the reconstituted SIT was to have been conducted by a three-member committee of IPS officers to be assisted by an officer not less than the DIG level from the CBI. Satish Verma's role was to be limited to the extent that he was supposed to ensure that the SIT investigation does not unduly go adverse to Ishrat Jahan.

Hence, Verma had no right to question me. No authority. One of the reconstituted SIT members should have questioned me. This is purely as per orders of High Court dated 1.12.2011:

> 62. In view of the aforesaid observations and discussion, the following directions:-
>
> (a) Mr.R.R. Verma, Chairman of SIT (present) shall register another/fresh FIR on the basis of his final (8th) report to the effect that the alleged encounter is not found to be genuine and for causing death of the deceased and consequently for the alleged offences under IPC and other provisions of the relevant laws.
> HC-NIC Page 161 of 165 Created On Thu Jul 21 12:47:49 IST 2016
> CR.MA/15981/2010 162/165 JUDGMENT
>
> (b) The aforesaid FIR shall be filed by Mr RR Verma, Chairman, SIT with the CBI, having jurisdiction for the crimes committed in Gujarat State, within a period of two weeks from the date of pronouncement of the order and the same shall be registered by the concerned officer of CBI.
>
> (c) CBI shall thereafter take up the investigation at the earliest and shall make an attempt to complete the same at the earliest.

(d) CBI shall entrust the investigation to the team of its officers headed by an officer not below the rank of DIG. During the course of investigation, the said team of investigation shall be at liberty to take help/assistance of Mr.Satish Verma, IPS (1986 Batch, Gujarat Cadre), Member of the present SIT in order to get clues for investigation and further incidental aspects of the investigation. However, it is clarified that the final decision shall be of the CBI as HC-NIC Page 162 of 165 Created On Thu Jul 21 12:47:49 IST 2016 CR.MA/15981/2010 163/165 JUDGMENT referred to herein above.

(e) After the registration of FIR by the Chairman of SIT, the record of the investigation made by the SIT shall be handed over to CBI by the Chairman of SIT.Court Order

(f) After the registration of FIR and after handing over the entire record of SIT to CBI, appropriate report shall be submitted to this Court by the Chairman of SIT. It is only thereafter that the SIT shall stand dissolved.

(g) The State Government shall spare the service of Mr.Satish Verma as and when so desired or required by the CBI for helping the CBI to provide clues for further investigation or any other matter related thereto.

(h) Further investigation of C. R. No.8/2004 of Crime Branch Police Station shall be transferred to CBI, within one month after the registration of the FIR by CBI as directed herein above. The State Government

HC-NIC Page 163 of 165 Created On Thu Jul 21 12:47:49 IST 2016
CR.MA/15981/2010 164/165 JUDGMENT
shall issue appropriate orders/notification for such purpose. CBI thereafter shall file appropriate report based on conclusion of SIT as per its 8th Report in the concerned Court, but the full details and the relevant documents shall be produced only after investigation of the aforesaid another/fresh FIR is completed and appropriate Report is filed in the concerned Court for another/fresh FIR.

(i) It is also observed and directed that in the event during the course of investigation of the aforesaid another/fresh FIR or complaint vide C.R. No.8/2004 of Crime Branch Police Station, the CBI is required to take any action against any Member of SIT, the same shall not be taken without prior permission of this Court.

(j) All the record, reports and other material supplied by the SIT be sealed properly and be kept in safe custody of the Registrar General of this Court.
HC-NIC Page 164 of 165 Created On Thu Jul 21 12:47:49 IST 2016
CR.MA/15981/2010 165/165 JUDGMENT

63. All the aspects of present application shall get concluded as per the aforesaid directions ordered herein above save and except that on the aspect of consideration of the matter for initiation of action under the Contempt of Courts Act separate orders shall be passed by this Court.

(Jayant Patel, J.)

(Smt. Abhilasha Kumari, J. Vinod)

HC

Satish Verma had got me to come to Ahmedabad without the knowledge, perhaps, of the investigating SIT officials. As I waited in his chamber, I learnt that another State police officer, P Gurjar, was being harassed by Satish Verma around the same time in the adjacent room. She had submitted that first report, saying it was an 'encounter'. Further, while for two minutes, when I had respite to go to the rest room, I saw a simple man being physically slapped by the CBI team. The victim was some Madan or Manojbhai. He was the owner of some Shakti Garage in Surat. He too had been summoned to the SIT office to be questioned. Due to some hindrances he had been delayed. The CBI officials were upset because they had called him at 11:00 am and he had arrived late.

Later I came to know that the entourage of Ishrat Jahan, Javed Sheik and other two Pakistani nationals had come from Nashik to Surat enroute to Ahmedabad to accomplish their mission. Their car broke down at Surat. They got the car repaired at this Shakti Garage. Monoj Siddhpura was the owner of this garage. Basically, as per information, they left Surat about 9:00 pm. They took seven-eight hours to cover a distance of about 270 km and reached the outskirts of Ahmedabad in the early hours of the morning. After they were accosted, the crossfire took place.

After a lot of acrimony with Verma, I was dropped at the airport that evening. I took an evening flight to Delhi. On 24.6.2013, I filed a report with my seniors. I had only submitted the report to my seniors in the Urban Development Division. I learnt that this report was placed before the Secretary (Urban Development). It was later sent to Union Home Secretary. Contents of this report are now available all over the net.

One thing that happened in the aftermath was not very pleasant. I was being chased by unknown people again. On the personal front, every acquaintance including many colleagues no longer mingled with me. Very few answered my calls, that too on landline. Then my immediate senior, M Ahmed, who was a sympathiser of the victim started berating me on every occasion.

He manipulated the first dispute against me on 7.8.2013. There was a case in which the department had to convey the position to a lawyer as to what is the land rate in respect of a particular parcel of land. The policy in this regard is that the highest of the DDA rates would be taken into account, some zonal rate or circle rate would be considered and of course, the ruling rate in the market. Stating this policy position, I had asked the technical division, which is the repository of this information what was to be conveyed. The response from them was 'x- rate is Rs.xxxx per sq. mtrs'. My natural conclusion was that this was the highest and applicable rate, as per the policy. But it was not and I was framed for this mistake.

Thereafter another case of dispute was opened. In this case, there was some confusion regarding a succession chain and I had sought the opinion of the Law Ministry and based on their input, I had taken a decision. Here the L&DO's refrain was, why did I consult the Law Ministry?

A third dispute was soon contrived. In this case, the Chief Architect (who was senior to the L&DO) under the same Ministry and local municipality had recommended change of land use in a certain dispute. On the downward journey from the Chief Architect, the file had been seen by me and I amended the lease conditions, based on this recommendation. But this was also called into question.

After so many disputes surfacing, I thought, Ahmed, the Joint Secretary and Khalid Bin Jama, Minister Kamal Nath's PS, were trying to cook my goose.

At the same time, I found a Deputy Superintendent of Police from the CBI, a man named Jayant Kashmiri, landing up in my office regularly on every Wednesday, which is marked for the public grievance redressal. On the first day when he appeared, I asked him what was his case? He introduced himself and said, *Director sahib ka kaam hai*. When I wanted to know, *aisa kya case hai*, he said it did not pertain to this office. Thereafter, every Wednesday afternoon, he would come to my room, occupy the chair opposite and not allow me to function. He would also inform all and sundry that he was from the CBI and try to damage my reputation. This fellow was also chasing me outside the office, which I learnt later.

There were other related unhappy incidents happening in my life. My son had settled down in the auto sector in Chennai with a job with a prominent automobile group. Even as a beginner, he was doing very well. It is a matter on the records of the corporate group. One fine day, my wife received a call from him. He appeared very upset. He had been asked to resign. No reasons were assigned. The top management personnel had called him up and asked him to resign. Accordingly, he submitted his resignation and was relieved on 14.12.2013. He told us, a colleague from the organisation had told him that it was to do with the CBI! We did not know the CBI had jurisdiction over private sector employment, or that it is mandated to intimidate kids, unconnected with parents' jobs. He returned to Delhi, very upset. He soon found another job in the automobile sector again, where he had made a name for himself. However, CBI harassment did not end with this.

In December 2013, my mother was staying with us. My wife was away in office that Saturday morning. This DSP of the CBI, Kashmiri landed in my house. Being an extremely foggy morning, we were all huddled in the inside room. This fellow came with his staff or goons (I do not know). They created a ruckus. They started throwing things in the sitting room. This totally traumatised my mother who was 87 years old. Their voices, their demeanour—everything about this DSP and his team was repulsive. That day my mother collapsed out of shock and tension. After many trips to the ISIC hospital and after we moved her away from my house, away from the bad memories, she died on 24.1.2014.

The long shadow of the Ishrat Jahan case

I resumed office from 24.2.2014. Again, pressure on me began to be applied in a subtle manner. The general elections to the Lok Sabha were coming up in May. The incumbent government wanted me to change my statement in the Ishrat Jahan case.

I was being asked to admit that Joint Director (IB), Rajinder Kumar, had brought a counter-affidavit, which I had signed and filed in the Gujarat High Court as a government affidavit, saying the government agreed with the initial Gujarat Police reports. Otherwise, the four people killed in the Ishrat Jahan encounter, including the two Pakistani terrorist, were paragons of virtue.

My only refrain was that the MHA (CBI and or any other MHA agency) should produce a document to say that there was no encounter and counter the earlier documents and I would sign the new document.

I had taken a similar stand in 2009. Rather my stand has always been that. In 2004, the JeD mouthpiece *Ghazwa Times* claimed Ishrat was a fidayeen. Later, when I said this, the same mouthpiece said 'she is a victim'.[20] The political advantage of this case was to be reaped by one entity. Was there any arrangement, understanding or some such thing in place?

There was a case of denotification of waqf land in Delhi which was going on for some time. The then British government had acquired this waqf land through the Land Acquisition Act of the time between 1912-1915. The incumbent government wanted to denotify the entire acquisition process after 100 years,

---

20 https://www.hindustantimes

in 2012-13, and give the land back to the Delhi Waqf Board.

The proposal was first rejected by Attorney General Goolam Vahanvati. Later, a proposal to review the opinion was sent to the AG. There was pressure on the AG from members of the Central Waqf Council, Rehman Khan, Minister of Minority Affairs and Kamal Nath, Minister for Urban Development. The AG changed his view. A proposal based on the revised legal opinion was placed before the Cabinet and got approved.

Since it takes a while for the minutes to be issued, I said, I would sign the denotification order only after the minutes confirming the decision was available on the file. As an interim measure, a letter was obtained from the concerned Secretariat confirming the decision. On 5 March 2014, as I was leaving the office, I was called by the Joint Secretary. He took me to the room of the Minister for Urban Development. I was told to toe the line by the Minister's PS, Khalid. The speaker phone was kept on for me to hear the Minister. There were two specific instructions from the Minister. Sign the denotification order which I had no problem doing because now I had written orders. I signed at about 9:00 pm that night. The second was a reiteration that I must toe the line.

While driving back home, I found myself being chased again. It was dark and I could hardly recognise the faces. But two to three vehicles were following me. At the Dwarka flyover at the top, where there is quite a lot of illumination, when one of the cars chasing me drew parallel to me, I could see a known face. He was the same personnel who had come with CBI DSP Jayant Kashmiri, and they had caused my mother to collapse. I do not know whether showing his face was an intentional pressure tactic. I was nevertheless apprehensive. Next day, the General Elections 2014 for the Lok Sabha was notified. The notification was for a 7-phase poll. This meant that till the elections were over, my travails would continue.

In the same period, my father had started missing my mother. He had been living with my sister-in-law, who would leave in the morning for her office. Later, he realised that he had a problem. He could not lock a house. This upset him and he was hurt psychologically. So I decided to be with him. This was the first time, I was to spend any time with him in 54 years. So I applied for leave on email from 6 March 2014. There was no recovering for my father though. And for me, there was no respite from the CBI.

On Sunday mornings, I visit the Sree Vinayaka Mandir in Sarojini Nagar for reciting and offering pranaams to the Surya God. This is the vedic suryanamaskara, contained in the Krishna Yajurveda known as Aruna Prasna. I was in my traditional attire. I was doing circumambulation of the deity after my regular ritual routine got over.

At this juncture, one gentleman approached me and said he wanted to talk to me. When I told him that I am not the priest of the temple and any religious queries had to be addressed to the priest, he told me that Archana Ramasundaram, IPS who was going to be Special Director, CBI had come to the temple and wanted to meet me. During those days, the appointment of this Special Director, CBI was making news with the Supreme Court being seized of the matter.

I reiterated that the lady could always consult the priest on religious matters and I was not the right person. The go-between insisted that I should speak to her. I thought she was seeking some VIP treatment. So I said that in this temple, even Supreme Court Judges, top functionaries of government, High Court Judges do visit and no VIP treatment is extended to anyone.

This gentleman still insisted that I speak to this CBI Special Director. While talking, we had together walked towards the place where the Homan (Havan) is performed. I told the go-between I would change my attire and come. From the staff quarters side, I exited after changing. I called my wife out on the mobile and we left the temple. I straight away drove to my childhood friend and lawyer K B B Singh's house. He calmed my nerves and thereafter, I drove back home.

My lawyer friend advised me to go missing for some time. Hence, I took a train, the Chennai Rajdhani, around the last week of March 2014 and went to Chennai. I stayed overnight in the IRCTC accommodation. The next morning I could not decide what to do. I went over to an old friend's place so that I could be diverted and had time to gather myself.

On the same evening, I took a train to Kumbakonam. Why Kumbakonam I do not know. Surely I can be unidentified in this place which I was visiting for the first time, I thought. I checked into a hotel opposite to the station. I would only call my wife from a local STD booth. Not access internet or email. Kumbakonam was a very inexpensive place. So the cash I carried was sufficient to cover my expenses for the period. I spent the time visiting many famous temples in the area. Later, when my money was over, I took the same route back to Chennai. I borrowed money from my friend and bought a tatkal ticket back to Delhi.

The last leg of the general elections got concluded in the first week of May 2014. I resumed my duty. Finally, on 15 May 2014, the election results were announced which is part of India's history. I was undergoing my annual medical examination at the Ram Manohar Lohia Hospital as the results were pouring in. There was excitement all around. In the afternoon, my colleague who was with me, told me that he was going back to office. I dropped him in Nirman Bhavan and drove back home.

I wanted to enjoy the feeling of relief. At least, the end of my travails was in sight. My wife, who had suffered with me, also needed to relax now. Actually during the marriage, the 2nd Vow taken in Sanskrit is *Dwitiyamcha Oorja Vishnu Anvetu*.

meaning the woman in the relationship shall be the epitome of the energy/power required for sustenance. In all these years she had epitomised that vow, she had been a great source of strength to me, otherwise I would have been lost long ago.

For me *Achhe Din* appeared to be beginning.

Still under the MHA's shadow

THE NEW GOVERNMENT was sworn in. There were high expectations. Interestingly, many friends who had shunned and spurned me all the previous years started calling me and asking about my welfare. They wanted to renew their contacts with me. I was not sure. In the meantime, I had also moved to the Ministry of Textiles.

In December 2013, one of police officers accused of Human Rights violation in the Ishrat Jahan case, N K Amin of the Gujarat cadre had filed a Criminal Writ Petition (No. 128/2013) in the Supreme Court.

The Supreme Court had issued a notice to me. This I received with a note from the Law Ministry with the instructions that MLJ (Minister for Law and Justice) would want to peruse the content of what I was to respond. Somehow, I could not find time to frame the response in consultation with my lawyer. The case was listed for 4.7.2014. I was present in the Court. I was directed to file my response in one month.

My response was ready by 5.8.2014 but due to procedural issues raised by Satish Verma's lawyer, I could not file my response. Finally, the response was filed on 7.8.2014. Extracts of my response is:

MANI RESPONDENT NO.6

I, R.V.S. Mani, son of Shri K.R.Ramaswamy aged about 54 years, resident of 139, DIN Apartments, Sector 4, Plot No. 7, Dwarka, New Delhi, do herby solemnly affirm and declare as...

under:-

1. The deponent is respondent No.6 in the above said writ petition and is aware of the facts and circumstances of the case pertaining to the averments made by the petitioner in respect of his acts performed by him during his tenure of his posting in Ministry of Home Affairs, Internal Security Division as Under Secretary. The deponent is also aware of some of the facts mentioned in the captioned petition: Being joined as a party respondent and having been served with the notice of this Hon'ble Court, the Deponent respectfully seeks to place the following facts on record:

3. That the deponent states that whatever he had stated in the affidavits dated 6.8.2009 and 29.9.2009 submitted by him before the Gujarat High Court were duly approved by the then Union Home Minister who had duly approved the same after examining the contents on record pertaining to the inputs given by respondent No.2.

4. That the deponent further states that during his tenure in such a sensitive assignment in the Home Ministry (Internal Security Wing), the inputs given by respondent No.2, were always found to be accurate, precise and professional which is evident from the detailed affidavit filed by the deponent on 6.8.2009 before the Hon'ble High Court of Gujarat.

In this context the deponent further submits that the deponent emphasized before the respondent No.7 who alone was interrogating the deponent reiterating his position that it was the domain of respondent No. 2 to give such inputs, which are processed at the highest level in the Ministry of Home Affairs before sharing the same with the respective state governments.

But the respondent No. 7 was adamant, rude, unruly and violent pressurising the deponent to state that one Shri Rajinder Kumar, IPS, the then Joint Director in the office of Respondent No. 2, had brought the draft affidavit' (subsequently filed before the Hon'ble Gujarat High Court) and the deponent has only it which is not true. In this context, the deponent further before the respondent No. (that he had also filed a similar affidavit in Allahabad High Court on 4.1.2008 when the High Court of Allahabad took suo motu notice as a sequel to terrorist attacks in District Courts in Uttar Pradesh on 22.11.2007. In that case also, the respondent No. 2 had given advance inputs about possible terror attacks in court premises in U.P, which the Union Home Ministry had shared with the Government of Uttar Pradesh on 16.10.2007 as well as 2.11.2007. The respondent No. 7 was violently adamant and he alleged that the officers like the deponent are stooges of respondent No. 2 and work under their dictates and did not take into account any thing based on facts shared by the deponent and continued to parrot his own version that the affidavit of 6.8.2009 was brought by Shri Rajinder Kumar, IPS and deponent simply signed it. The deponent was shocked and amazed by many things uttered by respondent No. 7 like terrorist attacks in Parliament was engineered by the ruling party in the Central Government then.

5. The deponent further states that on 22nd June, 2013 the deponent was called for recording of his statement by the CBI SIT. The deponent found that no officer interrogated the deponent but the deponent was interrogated by Shri Satish Verma, IPS, the respondent No.7 herein who tried to intimidate, coerce and even induce the deponent to sign on the dotted lines a statement as desired by him. Since deponent was in a post of responsibility and was well versed with the 4 facts mentioned in the affidavits, he did not succumb to the rude, violent and

intimidating torture of respondent No.7 and stuck to the true facts. Since the deponent underwent a serious and unprecedented physical and mental torture, the deponent decided to report the same to his seniors in the Ministry of Urban Development immediately upon his return from Gandhinagar to New Delhi in writing at the relevant point of time viz. contemporaneously on 24th June, 2013 since 23rd June, 2013 was Sunday. As per the information of the deponent, the said written note of the deponent was also contemporaneously forwarded by the Urban Development Ministry to the Home Ministry in June, 2013 itself. A copy of the said note is Annexed herewith and is annexed as ANNEXURE-1.

6. The deponent states that after the deponent filed the above referred note in the official records contemporaneously, as stated above, the deponent was mentally and administratively harassed continuously, However since the said facts may not have relevance with the subject matter of the present petition, the deponent is advised not to elaborate the same in this affidavit. However the deponent reserves liberty to place the same on record as and when so advised. That from the beginning viz, The deponent placing the note in the official records till now, the deponent was continuously called, chased and stalked by many senior CBI officers including one senior level lady IPS officer recently posted in the CBl.

7. The deponent states that the deponent is filing this affidavit only with a view to place the true and correct facts before this Hon'ble Court and has nothing to state so far as the prayers prayed for in the petition are concerned. Nothing from this Hon'ble Court,

Few days after this SC deposition, a letter was received in the office of my lawyer issuing a fatwa[21] to kill me. I submitted the same to my office. It was also submitted before the Supreme Court bench hearing the petition on 12.9.2014.

21 a religious ruling to kill

The then Joint Secretary (Administration), Sujit Gulati, a lovely and a friendly officer, seemed more disturbed than I was. He spoke to the Joint Secretary in the MHA and forwarded the letter to them. After this, the MHA and Delhi Police did a good job of assessing the threat to me. The Delhi Police wanted me to tell them what kind of security I wanted, they had assessed that the 'threat was imminent' and had to make some mitigating recommendations. I, however, did not want to be bogged by the paraphernalia of PSOs, so I declined the offer of bodyguards in writing.

Meanwhile, my sister-in-law had been transferred to Ranchi. My father felt he would get a change of place as he was yet to really recover from the loss of my mother, with whom he had spent nearly 70 years. The letters received at her Delhi residence were redirected to her Ranchi home. Without anyone's knowledge about the content, a white envelope also got redirected to the Ranchi home. My father opened it to find inside a copy of the same *fatwa* received at my lawyer's office. The entire process of postal delivery and redirection etc. had taken two more months in time. My father saw the *fatwa* in November 2014. Few days later, he fell ill and was admitted to a hospital.

My wife and I had to go in December 2014 to Ranchi and bring him back to Delhi in a semi-conscious state. We admitted him to a Delhi hospital again. After his discharge a few days later, he lived practically as a vegetable, coming to his senses only intermittently.

Meanwhile, several interesting but worrisome incidents kept on happening to me. I would find the nuts of all the four wheels of my vehicle loosened while it was parked in the office parking lot.

Then, one night, after a get-together at my lawyer friend's house in south Delhi where we were meeting a few other old friends, when I was driving home, suddenly from the midst of a

FATWA/ DIKTAT

(Translated from Arabic)

In the name of ALLAH

Resolved on this solemn date of which is 22.8.2014 after Juma-e-Namaz(Friday Prayers)

A question was posed to Ulema about one Dr R.V.S. Mani who has filed an Affidavit in the Supreme Court on 19.8.2014 accusing Ishrat Jehan and her other accompanying persons as terrorist.

Dr. R.V.S. Mani, also in his affidavit has praised the virtue of Intelligence Officers and Gujarat Police Officers who were involved in killing young Islamic volunteers

Dr. R.V.S Mani, had while in Home Ministry also had reported Delhi Police who killed your Muslim students in Delhi on 19 September 2008 in Batla House, Shaheen Bagh, Jamia Nagar, New Delhi. He declared the Delhi Police Special Officers innocent. This Academy cannot forgive the Delhi Police for some of boys killed were our volunteers

Dr. R.V.S. Mani also made some reports due to which many of our boys could not get transit remand to Delhi from Gujarat Jails where these boys were being tortured, by the tyrannical Government of Modi and Amit Shah.

By his action Dr. R.V.S Mani has betrayed that he is agent of Modi and Amit Shah.

Dr. R.V.S. Mani, when posted in Ministry of Urban Development, always created hurdles in work of Islamic Organisation/ or Muslim organisation relating land allotment to Muslim organisation, demolition of mosques in Netaji Nagar, de notification of Waqf Properties, Khilafat with Mr. Mahmood Ahmed, Land & Development Officer, and Mr. Jamal-Khalid-Bin, some bright officers of our community, who were helping our organisations

This assembly orders the faithfuls to kill Dr.R.V.S. Mani whose actions can cause danger to Islam.

metro construction site a dumper appeared. It was on the wrong side of the road. It came in front of my car and crashed into it. The entire front portion of my vehicle was damaged. Miracle was that I did not get a scratch on my body.

My father was living with another brother of mine in Delhi at the time. He learnt of these attacks on me and his condition worsened. Five days later he died. He was 92. Just a few months ago he could travel independently to any destination for performing Bhagwat Saptaham or Chandi pooja. He was in great demand. An erudite person, he still had a few years left in him. But the fallout of my professional life took his life. He died a very traumatised human being.

Unto the Sun

But things did not stop here. In February 2016, due to online recording of statements by David Headley in the Abu Jundal trial, many unknown details of the Ishrat Jahan case came into the public domain. The media's quest to learn the truth, bare the facts in the various terrorism cases intensified. After they had spoken to Rajinder Kumar and former Home Secretary, G K PIllai, the *Times Now* television channel landed up at my residence. My story was aired on *Times Now* on 1 March 2016.

I always desired to be an anonymous common man. But this media exposure brought me into limelight. I was apprehensive and went and confessed to Secretary, Ministry of Textiles, that I had given this interview. Rashmi Verma, the then Secretary, Ministry of Textiles, at first berated me for being tactless. But she was an excellent professional and an understanding human being who extended all support in this regard.

Even after the government changed and I was on television, my harassment continued. In April, I received a legal notice from one Srivastava, a Supreme Court lawyer—sent by a lawyer named Rachna Gupta dated 1.4.2016—about some special treatment not being extended to him in the Sree Vinayaka Mandir, of which I was associated in the management. While I did not reply to this, later inquiries revealed that it was Satish Verma's way of getting at me, Srivastava was his relative.

One evening, when I was returning home, at the Dwarka Flyover, a car went past my car, from the left side. It was dark and hence I could not make out the finer details. The driver pulled out a gun and threatened me, abusing me with the choicest Punjabi abuses and said he would kill me. I called the Delhi Police Control Room, and later a policeman came to my house and recorded the details including the car number which I had noted down. Police later told me, the man was Vipul Kwatra, living in Sector 12, Dwarka and had a licensed firearm. No clue to why the man had suddenly waved his gun at me. I was definitely rattled.

In the Textile Ministry, I had contributed to the Mobile App in the name of 'eDhaga' for the benefit of handloom weavers. The App is targeted to benefit about 4 lakh weavers attached to the 932 government depots in 30 States/UTs. Being from the Central Secretariat Service I am not entitled to apply for any recognition for this, but I felt, I deserved government recognition. I soon began to feel disaffected with my lot.

I had to do a certain amount of travelling. Generally, I prefer to stay in government guest houses, especially in Mumbai. On 22.4.2017, I had to attend a meeting in Mumbai in the Churchgate area. This was followed by a visit to one of our organisations in the Wool Research Association at Thane on 23rd April. I was staying in the Textiles Committee Guest House at Prabhadevi. On the night of the 22nd, after the meeting was over, I reached the Guest House, changed and went over to a dhabha near Dadar Station, which is one of my favourite places for good Punjabi khana. I returned to the guest house around 11:00 pm and went off to sleep, planning for a early morning aarti-time visit to the Siddivinayaka temple.

At about 1:30 am. the entire power supply of the guest house went off. It was pitch dark. After struggling and locating my mobile, I tried opening the door of my room and found it locked from the outside. I called up one of the officers who lived in the complex. He sent someone who quietly unbolted the door and went away. I struggled to go towards the terrace area and fell down. At the time I could feel someone pressing my neck with force. I kicked my legs aimlessly and my attacker ran away, leaving me in a semiconscious state.

Later, when I had gained my composure, I called the officer again, vacated the guest house around 3:00 am. and after scouting around for a hotel, checked myself in at a hotel in Worli. I used my wife's spouse card to make the payment. When she received the card message in the early hours of the morning, she was paranoid as she had suffered a lot of trauma in the previous years.

I returned to Delhi during the day and told her about the attack on me in the guest house. It was obvious people hostile to me were keeping tabs on my movements. She urged K B B Singh, my advocate and childhood friend, to take action and he did send a notice in this regard.

In a popular movie of the last decade, *Wednesday*, the lead actor, Naseeruddin Shah, complains that his wife calls up every now and then seeking to know whether he had had his tea etc., but the real intent is to confirm whether he is safe and not a victim of any untoward incident. My predicament is no different. After calculating how long it would take to go wherever I was going, my wife now calls me to confirm whether I have reached safely.

Epilogue

I was fed up of serving the government. After a great deal of brainstorming with family and friends, I decided to take Voluntary Retirement from Service. After all, I had hit a glass ceiling.

In conclusion, some thoughts for India's political leadership. My father would always say, refer to the holy *Bhagwad Gita* as a life management tool. Whenever someone was in difficulty, he would advice reference to the *Gita* to find solutions in its verses.

In the last seven decades the leadership has brought the nation to such a pass, it is in difficult times. India's social fabric is being torn to threads. My sincere suggestion as a citizen of this great country of mine to all persons who wear the mantle of leadership, who are striving for the nation's leadership, who are under the illusion that they are leading the country, refer to the following verse from *Bhagwad Gita*:

> Yad Yad carati shrestatha tad tad evatoro janah
> Sa yat pramanam kurute, lokas tad anuvartate

A leader's (shretada yad yad kurute) acts are followed by common people, proof (pramanam kurute) of a leader's outstanding acts is that it is followed world over.

Please make your actions such that they are idealistic and meaningful to be followed world over; strive to go by the above ideals and refrain from acting in any manner which, followed by common people, could tear the values enshrined in the Constitution and its Preamble to shreds.

Last word, I will die only once. My detractors may make thousand attempts. I will not succumb to any pressure, intimidation, fear etc. After all, my mother always branded me as a fearless person. I cannot betray her.

Annexures from the Indo-Pak Dossier

Navigation map of the sea route found with terrorists

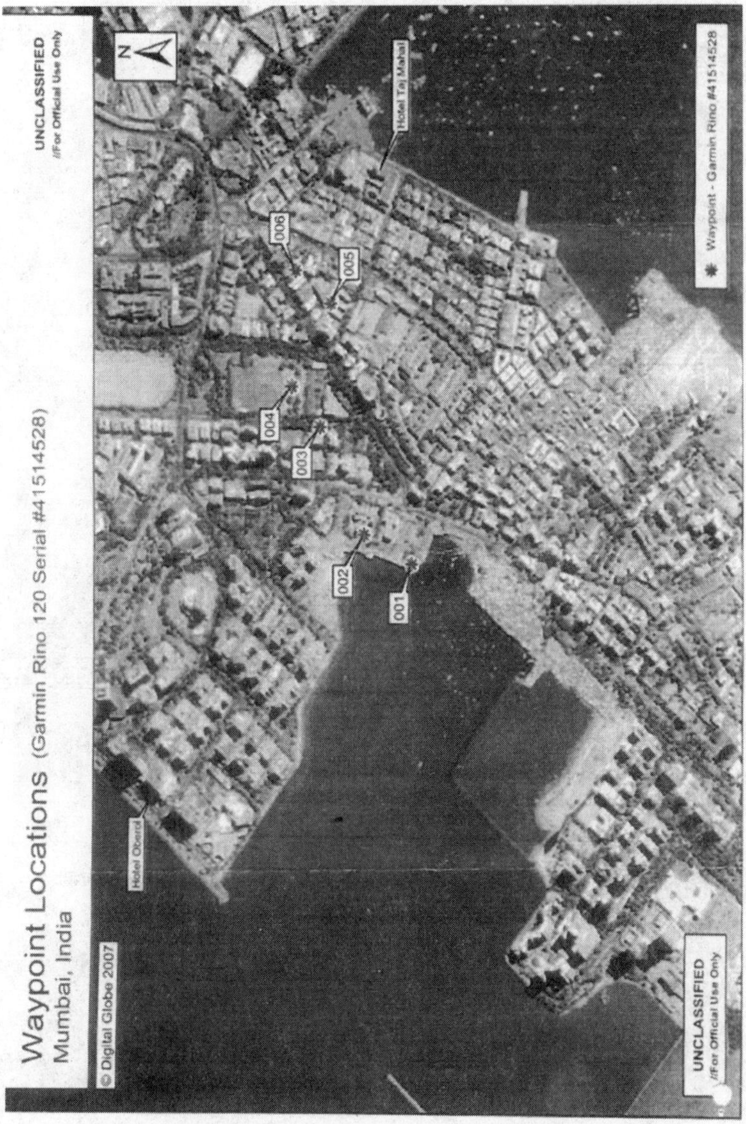
Waypoint Locations (Garmin Rino 120 Serial #41514528)
Mumbai, India
UNCLASSIFIED
//For Official Use Only
© Digital Globe 2007
N
Hotel Oberoi
Hotel Taj Mahal
001
002
003
004
005
006
Waypoint - Garmin Rino #41514528
UNCLASSIFIED
//For Official Use Only

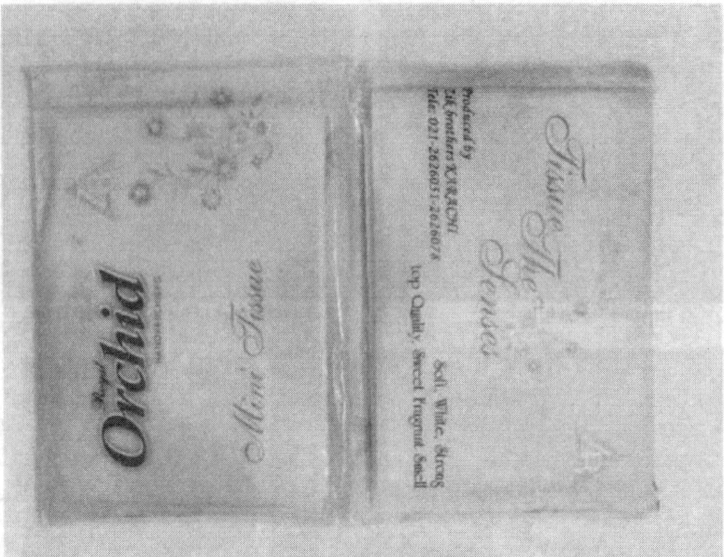

Tissue paper – Made in Pakistan

Wheat flour-Made in Pakistan

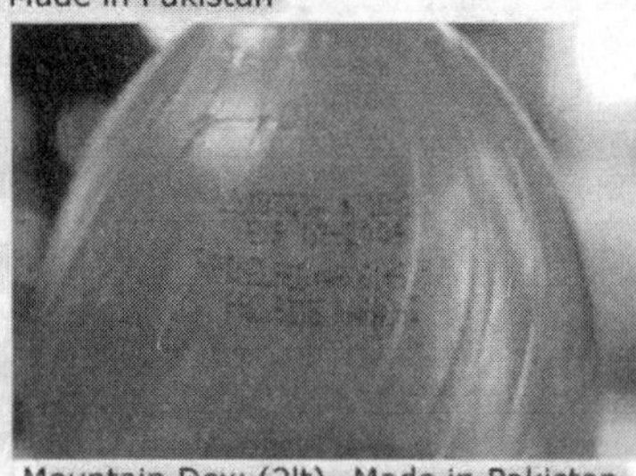
Mountain Dew (2lt)- Made in Pakistan

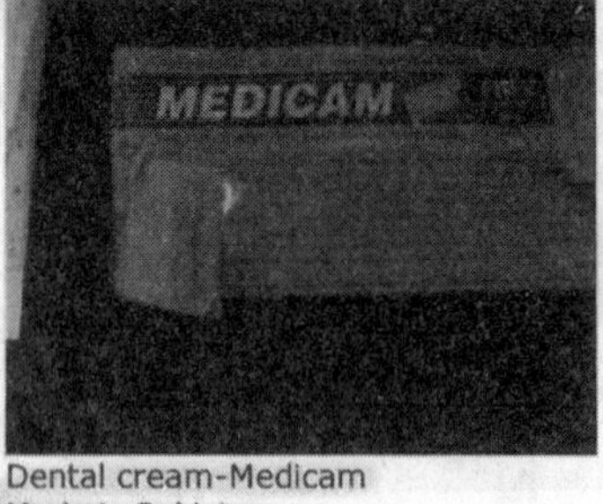

Dental cream-Medicam
Made in Pakistan

Shaving cream-Touchme
Made in Pakistan

Sogo Spray paint-Made in Pakistan

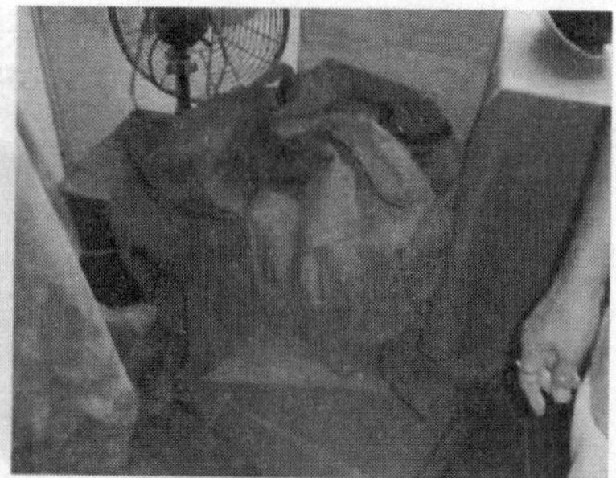

Yamaha engine cover

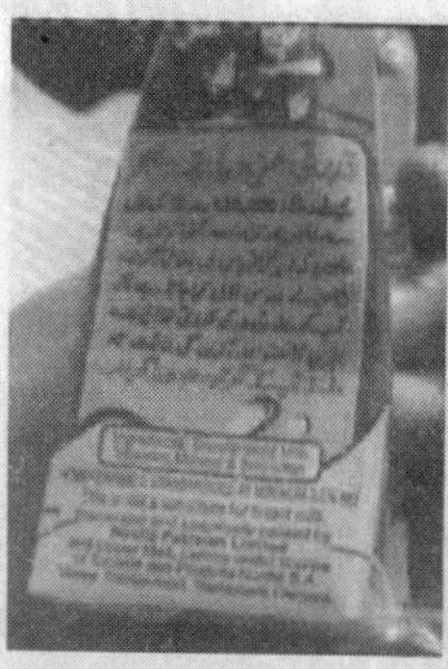

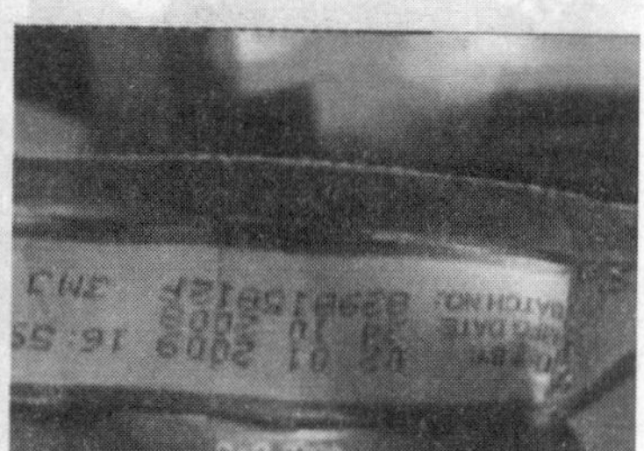

Made in Pakistan milk powder packets (Nestle)

GPS

GPS recovered from Kuber

GPS recovered from Nariman House

GPS recovered from the Taj Mahal palace

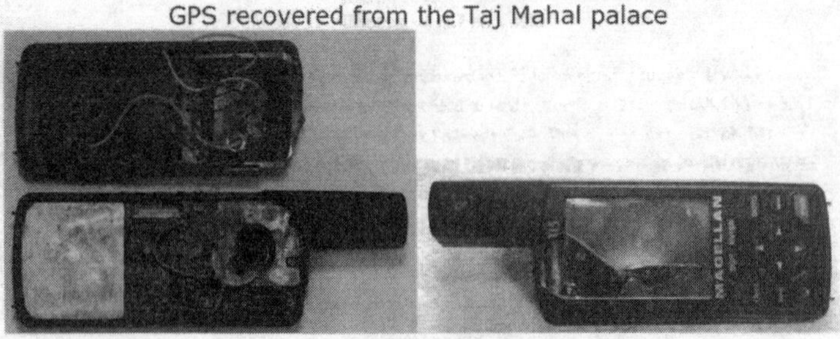

Section II Dossier

II. Pak response to Mumbai attacks

Pakistani leaders and Officials after the attack on Mumbai made different statements that indicate continuous prevarication.

January 09 Ministry of External Affairs 60

Visit of DG, ISI to India

- **Initial position**: On 28 Nov 2008, Pakistan PMO and FO issued Press Releases that DG ISI would visit India.
- **Changed Position**: Later on, on 28th Nov 2008 night a spokesman for Prime Minister's House said that a representative of the Inter-Services Intelligence (ISI) will visit India instead of the Director General.

  On 30 Nov 2008, President Zardari said in an interview: "There was a miscommunication. We had announced that a director will come from my side. That is what was requested by the (Indian) prime minister and that is what we agreed".

January 09 Ministry of External Affairs 61

Air Space violation and Military Buildup

- On 13 Dec 2008, PM Gilani said it was a minor technical mistake. Information Minister Sherry Rehman said it was inadvertent.
- On 14 Dec 2008, President Zardari said it was a technical mistake
- On 18 Dec 2008 Pakistan conveyed its concern on technical and air space violations by Indian aircraft alleged on 12 and 13 December 2008.
- Airspace violation was denied by India on 13.12.2008 itself.

January 09 Ministry of External Affairs 62

Kasab's Identity and Involvement of Pakistani Nationals

- A **Sunday Observer Newspaper report on 7/12/08 has established that the lone surviving gunman** caught by Indian police during last week's terrorist attacks on Mumbai came **from Faridkot village in the Okara district of the Pakistani Punjab**
- On 13 Dec 2008, GEO TV reported that when Ajmal Kasab's father was shown the pictures published in newspapers after Mumbai attacks, he confirmed that the man in the picture was his son.
- On 9 Dec 2008, PR of Pakistan to UN at UNSC said that i) the Government of Pakistan has already initiated investigations on its own pertaining to the allegations of involvement of persons and entities in Mumbai ii) an intelligence led operation strongly supported by law enforcement agencies is already underway to arrest the individuals alleged to be involved in the Mumbai attacks.

January 09 Ministry of External Affairs 63

Kasab's Identity and Involvement of Pakistani Nationals (2)

Changed position

- On 17 Dec 2008 Pakistan's High commissioner to India, Shahid Malik said that Ajmal Kasab is not a Pakistani citizen.
- On 17 Dec 2008, President Zardari in an Interview to BBC said that there is still no proof that the gunmen who attacked Mumbai came from Pakistan

January 09 Ministry of External Affairs 64

Home Secretaries' Talks 10-11Aug, 2004

- Details of 20 major incidents of terror in Jammu and Kashmir and other parts of India caused by Pakistan based /ISI sponsored terrorist outfits.
- Details of 21 major terrorist modules busted in various parts of India revealing involvement of Pakistan based/ISI sponsored terrorist outfits.
- List of 12 known training camps in Pakistan /Pakistan occupied Kashmir used by terrorist outfits along with map.
- List of 31 communication control stations in Pakistan/Pakistan occupied Kashmir used by terrorist outfits along with maps.
- List along with details of **25** most wanted fugitives from law in India who are residing in Pakistan.
- Sample cases showing involvement of ISI and Pak nationals in circulation of Fake Indian Currency Notes (FICNs)into India.
- List of 257 Pakistani nationals and foreign mercenaries killed in Jammu and Kashmir as claimed by terrorist outfits based in Pakistan/Pakistan occupied Kashmir.

January 09 Ministry of External Affairs 71

Home Secretaries' Talks
29-30th August , 2005

- **List along with details of most wanted fugitives from law in India who are residing in Pakistan:** Dawood Ibrahim Kaskar @ Shaikh Dawood Hasan @ Dawood Sabri (Indian), Memon Ayub Abdul Razak (Indian), Memon Ibrahim @ Tiger @ Mushtaq @ Sikander (Indian), Shaikh Shakeel @ Chhota Shakeel (Indian), Ibrahim Athar @Ahmed Ali Mohd Ali Sheikh @ Siddiqui Javed @ Chief @ AA Sheikh @ Ibrahim (PAK),Azhar Yusuf @ Mohd. Salim (PAK), Mistri Zahur Ibrahim @ Bhola (PAK), Sayeed Shahid Akhtar @ Doctor @ Moti Khalid (PAK), Shakir Md. @ Shankar @ Rajesh Gopal Verma@ Ram Gopal Verma @ Farooq Abdul Aziz Siddiqi (PAK), Ishaq Atta Hussain @ Ali Moosa (Indian), Sagir Sabir Ali Shaikh (Indian), Maulana Mohammad Masood Azhar Alvi @ Maulana Masood Azhar @ Vali Adam Isa (PAK), Mohd. Yusuf Shah @ Salauddin (Indian), Gajinder Singh @ GAjinder Singh Khalsa (Indian), Lakhbir Singh @ Singh Lakhbir Rode@ Singh Lakhbir (Indian), Paramjit Singh Panjwar @ Paramjit Pamma @ Gian Singh (Indian), Ranjit Singh @ Manpreet Singh @ Neeta (Indian), Wadhawa Singh (Indian), Anwar Ahmed Haji Jamal Theba (Indian), Anis Ibrahim Kaskar Shaikh (Indian),Mohammad Ahmed Dosa (Indian), Amanullah Khan (PAK), Aftab Batki (PAK), Abdul Rauf (PAK), Javed Patel@ Javed Chikna @ Javed Dawood Tailor (Indian),Karimulla Habib Shaikh (Indian), Slaim Abdul Gani Gazi (Indian), Riyaz Abu Bakar Khatri (Indian), Munaf Abdul Majid Halari (Indian), Mohd. Tainur Mohd. Phansopkar Salim Mujahid (Indian).

January 09 | Ministry of External Affairs | 72

Home Secretaries' Talks
30-31st May, 2006

- Details of recent major incidents of terror in J&K and other parts of India caused by Pakistan /Pakistan occupied Kashmir-based/ISI sponsored terrorist outfits.
- Details of recent major terrorist modules neutralised in various parts in India revealing involvement of Pakistan/Pakistan occupied Kashmir-based/ ISI sponsored terrorist outfits.
- Profile of a ISI element involved in narcotic smuggling and pushing in of fake Indian currency for terrorist actions.
- List of known major training camps in Pakistan / Pakistan occupied Kashmir and Northern Areas used by terrorist outfits along with maps.
- List of communication Control Stations in Pakistan/ Pakistan occupied Kashmir used by terrorist outfits along with map.
- List (of 35) along with details of most wanted fugitives from law in India who are residing in Pakistan.
- List of Pakistan and foreign mercenaries recently killed/ arrested in India.

January 09 | Ministry of External Affairs | 73

Foreign Secretaries' 14-15th Nov, 2006

- **Document handed over by Indian Foreign Secretary to Pakistan Foreign Secretary on 14th November, 2006 regarding Pakistan links to :**
- Varanasi twin blasts on March 7, 2006
- Delhi Serial Blasts on October 29, 2005.
- Suicide bombing at STF office, Hyderabad on Oct 12, 2005.
- Terrorist attack at Ayodhya on July 5, 2005

January 09 Ministry of External Affairs 74

I Meeting of JATM 6th March, 2007

- **Details of 35 Red Corner Notice Subjects residing in Pakistan already shared with the Pakistani side at Home Secretary Talks on Counter Terrorism and Drug Trafficking (30th -31st May, 2006).**
- **A document containing details of following 12 cases was handed over:**

Deportation of Mohammad Faisal Naeem from Bangladesh to Pakistan.
Haren Pandya murder case
Explosions in public transport buses in Ahmedabad.
Suicide bombing at Special Task Force (Hyderabad Police) office
Recovery of arms, ammunition and explosives in Aurangabad
Fidayeen attack on Congress rally in Srinagar.
Grenade attacks on tourists in Srinagar
Violence carried out by Mohammad Amin Baba of Hizb-ul-Mujahideen
Planting of improvised explosive devices in Baramulla, J&K
Attack on security forces at Boniyar, Baramulla, J&K
Escape of Ghulam Rasool Shah from police custody.
Serial blasts in Mumbai local trains

January 09 Ministry of External Affairs 75

Home Secretaries' Talks
3 – 4 July, 2007

- Details of recent major incidents of terror in J&K and other parts of India caused by terrorist outfits based in Pakistan/ Pakistan occupied Kashmir.
- Details of recent major terrorist modules exposed in J&K and other parts of India revealing involvement of terrorist outfits based in Pakistan/Pakistan occupied Kashmir
- Specific cases of involvement of elements in Pak Intelligence establishment in fomenting anti-India activities including terrorism, narcotic smuggling, circulation of FICN, etc.
- List of known major training camps in Pakistan /Pakistan occupied Kashmir & Northern Areas used by terrorist outfits along with maps.
- List of Communication Control Stations in Pakistan/Pakistan occupied Kashmir used by terrorist outfits along with map.
- List along with details of most wanted fugitives from law in India who are residing in Pakistan.
- List of Pakistani and other foreign terrorists recently killed/arrested and their involvement in terrorist activities in India.

January 09 | Ministry of External Affairs | 76

II Meeting of JATM
22nd Oct, 2007

- **Document handed over by India containing information based on interrogation on the following**: Muhammad Younas @ Bilal of Lashkar-e-Tayyaba, Abdullah @ Asgar Ali of Lashkar-e-Tayyaba Muzaffar Ahmed Rather @ Rafi of Lashkar-e-Tayyaba, Muhammad Bilal@ Zubair of Jaish-e-Muhammad, Adnan Younis Bhatti@ Muhammad Sohail Afzal of Jaish-e-Muhammad, Jalaluddin Mulla@ Babu Bhai of Harkat-ul-Islami, Muhammad Naushad of Harkat –ul-Jehad-al-Islami, Nasir Hussain of Harkat-ul-Jehad-al-Islami, Muhammad Yaqub of Harkat-ul-Jehad-al-Islami, Sheikh Mukhtar Hussain of Harkat-ul-Jehad-al-Islami, Muhammad Ali Akbar Hussain of Harkat-ul-Jehad-al-Islami, Muhammad Yasin @ Abu Saraka of Lashkar-e-Tayyaba, Akhtar Teli @ Akhtar-al-Islam of Lahkar-e-Tayyaba, Mubarak Ahmed Wani of Hizb-ul-Mujahideen.
- **Information gathered in the investigations of the following events**: Attack on Mangat Ram Sharma (ex-Dy.CM) Srinagar on 13-07-2004, Terrorist attack on Prime Minister's meeting – Srinagar on 17-11-2004, Terrorist Attack on Bombay – Gujrat Hotel Srinagaron 29-07-2005, Terrorist attack on M.Y. Tarigami (MLA/CPM) and assassination of Ghulam Nabi Lone (Ex-MOS, Education) on 18-10-2005, Terrorist attack on CRPF Camp, Nageen, Srinagar, Terrorist attack on Firdaus Cinema Hall – Srinagar on 23-11-2005 and Robbery at J&K Bank in Srinagar on 30-11-2005.
- **A consolidated list of 48** (absconders wanted in Mumbai Blast Cases 1993 + Hijackers of IC-814 + Attackers of Parliament + Sikh Terrorists + Accused involved in illegal arms smuggling + Other activities) was handed over

January 09 | Ministry of External Affairs | 77

III Meeting of JATM
24th June, 2008

- **Document handed over containing information based on the interrogation of:** Imran Shahzad @ Abu Shama of Lashkar-e-Tayabba, Muhammad Farooq Bhatti @ Abu Zaar of Lashkar-e-Tayabba, Sabahuddin Ahmad @ Farhan of Lashkar-e-Tayabba, Muhammad Sharief @ Suhail of Lashkar-e-Tayabba involved in the **Attack on CRPF camp at Rampur – Januray 01, 2008**
- Nissar Ahmad Bhat @ Gazi Misbahuddi of Hizbul Mujahideen and Tajamul Islam @ Asif of Hizbul Mujahideen involved in the Terrorist strike by Lashkar-e-Tayabba (LeT) at Samba, J&K
- Muhammad Abid @ Safdar of Jaish-e-Muhammad, Saiful Rehman @ Yusuf Khan of Jaish-e-Muhammad, Mirza Rashid Beig @ Raja of Jaish-e-Muhammad involved in a **Plan to kidnap a political personality**
- Saqib Aziz Malik @ Abu Sayeed of Lashkar-e-Tayyaba, Tafeem Akmal Hashmi @ Feema of Al Badar, Qurban Ali @ Zubair of Hizbul Mujahideen and Zafar Iqbal Sudan@ Rehman of Jaish-e-Muhammad **involved in an explosion in Shrinagar Cinema Hall, Ludhiana, Punjab on 14-10-07**
- **List of terrorists of Lashkar-e-Tayyaba (LeT) killed in India** – as Claimed in JuD/ LeT periodicals.

January 09 | Ministry of External Affairs | 78

Special meeting of JATM
24-10-2008

- **Document handed over by India containing information based on the interrogation of**

  Karimullah Osain Khan @ Karimullah Habib of Dawood Ibrahim Gang (Karimulla has confirmed presence of 14 criminals accused in Bombay blasts in 1993 in Karachi, Pakistan)

  Raziuddin Nasir @ Abdul Rehman of Lashkar-e-Tayyaba (LeT)

  Muhammad Fahad @ Neduthanni @ Muhammad Koya of Al Badar

  Muhammad Ali Hussain @ Jehangir @ Kasim of Al Badar

  Muhammad Imran Butt @ Umar Saani of Lashkar-e-Tayyaba (LeT)

  Sikander Azam Sani Butt @ Abu Hurrera of Lashkar-e-Tayyaba (LeT)

  Muhammad Hashim Khan @ Darvesh of Harkat-ul-Mujahideen (HuM)
- **Leads on attack on Indian Embassy in Kabul on 7th July, 2008**

January 09 | Ministry of External Affairs | 79

Home Secretaries' Talks 25-26 Nov 2008

- Details of 32 Indian and 10 Pakistani fugitives and who are based in Pakistan handed over. The list contains the names of fugitives like Dawood Ibrahim, Masood Azhar, Tiger Memon, and others.

January 09 Ministry of External Affairs 80

Sample of Responses given by Pakistan to evidence shared during meetings

- Investigations so far have not yielded anything linked to attack on the Embassy being present in Pakistan (Special Session of JATM) in October 2008
- On the evidence given on statements and operations of JeM, LeT, JuD, the Pakistani response was that all these groups were banned or under watch in Pakistan.
- LeT & JeM have already been banned in Pakistan

January 09 Ministry of External Affairs 81

Section IV Dossier

IV. Pakistan's Commitments and Obligations

Bilateral, International, and Multilateral commitments obligate Pakistan to act against Terrorism emanating from its territory. These are listed in the following slides:

January 09 Ministry of External Affairs 83

Bilateral Commitments

- President Musharraf assured Prime Minister Vajpayee that he will not permit any territory under Pakistan's control to be used to support terrorism in any manner. **[Joint Statement of 6th January 2004]**
- President Zardari reassured Prime Minister Manmohan Singh that the Government of Pakistan stands by its commitments of January 6, 2004, not to permit any territory under Pakistan's control to be used to support terrorism in any manner. **[Joint Statement of 24th September 2008]**

January 09 Ministry of External Affairs 84

International Obligations

- **International convention for the Suppression of Terrorist Bombings, 1997.**
  - Article 2 makes it an offence to detonate an explosive in or against a place of public use, a state or govt. facility. Any person who participates as an accomplice is also covered as an offender.
  - Under Article 7 a State which receives information about such offender is required to take measures to ensure his presence for prosecution or extradition.
  - All persons who participated in or contributed to the terrorist attack are covered under this Convention.
  - Pakistan as a State Party is required to extradite or prosecute such offenders and also provide mutual legal assistance in investigation or prosecution.

January 09 Ministry of External Affairs 85

International Obligations

- International Convention Against the Taking of Hostages, 1979.
  - Applicable as the terrorists had taken hostages and murdered them later.
  - Pakistan as a State Party is obliged under this Convention to cooperate in investigations including extradition.

January 09 Ministry of External Affairs 86

MULTILATERAL OBLIGATIONS

- The SAARC Convention on Suppression of Terrorism, 1987
  - Mumbai attack is covered under it as a terrorist act.
  - The Convention requires States Parties to provide mutual legal assistance and has provisions for extradition.

January 09 Ministry of External Affairs 87

MULTILATERAL OBLIGATIONS

- Additional Protocol to the SAARC Convention on Suppression of Terrorism, 2004 [entered into force on 12th January 2006]
  - Has provisions related to suppression of financing of terrorism (similar to UN Terrorist Financing Convention).
  - Pakistan is required to take measures to freeze funds used for committing terrorist attacks.

January 09 Ministry of External Affairs 88

Section V Dossier

V. What Pakistan should do

This was a conspiracy launched from Pakistan. Gaps in knowledge can be filled by investigation and interrogation of conspirators there. Some of the actions that India expects Pakistan to undertake in extending cooperation to bring the terrorists to justice are listed in the following slide.

January 09 Ministry of External Affairs 90

What Pakistan should do (2)

- Handover conspirators to face justice in India.
- Handover fugitives from Indian law based in Pakistan.
- Dismantle infrastructure of Terrorism
- Prevent Terrorist acts from Pakistan.
- Adhere to and Implement bilateral, multilateral and international obligations.

January 09 Ministry of External Affairs 91

Hoax Call Issue

- Government of Pakistan Officials claimed that the President of Pakistan received a threatening call from the External Affairs Minister of India on 28-11-08. It subsequently emerged that the call was a hoax. Pakistan has however continued to harp on this to build up hysteria about India-Pakistan tensions.
- It has been clarified by our External Affairs Minister that:
- "My last and only conversation with President Zardari was in Islamabad during my May 2008 visit".
- "The only telephonic conversation with a Pakistani leader I had was on 28-11-08 with FM Pakistan in New Delhi".
- "I can only ascribe this to those in Pakistan, who wish to divert attention from the fact that a terrorist group operating from the Pakistani territory, planned and launched a ghastly attack on Mumbai".

January 09 Ministry of External Affairs 67

The controversy about Mukherjee and Zardari

ऑम् तत् सत्